MOLLY MAID
CLEANING
HANDBOOK

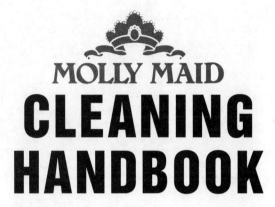

MOLLY MAID
CLEANING
HANDBOOK

The Complete Guide to a Clean House

MOLLY MAID EXPERTS

PENGUIN
CANADA

PENGUIN CANADA

Published by the Penguin Group

Penguin Group (Canada), 90 Eglinton Avenue East, Suite 700,
Toronto, Ontario, Canada M4P 2Y3
(a division of Pearson Canada Inc.)

Penguin Group (USA) Inc., 375 Hudson Street, New York, New York 10014, U.S.A.
Penguin Books Ltd, 80 Strand, London WC2R 0RL, England
Penguin Ireland, 25 St Stephen's Green, Dublin 2, Ireland
(a division of Penguin Books Ltd)
Penguin Group (Australia), 250 Camberwell Road, Camberwell, Victoria 3124,
Australia (a division of Pearson Australia Group Pty Ltd)
Penguin Books India Pvt Ltd, 11 Community Centre, Panchsheel Park,
New Delhi – 110 017, India
Penguin Group (NZ), 67 Apollo Drive, Rosedale, North Shore 0745,
Auckland, New Zealand (a division of Pearson New Zealand Ltd)
Penguin Books (South Africa) (Pty) Ltd, 24 Sturdee Avenue, Rosebank,
Johannesburg 2196, South Africa

Penguin Books Ltd, Registered Offices: 80 Strand, London WC2R 0RL, England

First published 2009

1 2 3 4 5 6 7 8 9 10   (WEB)

Copyright © MOLLY MAID International Inc., 2009

Manufactured in Canada.

ISBN: 978-0-14-317204-8

Library and Archives Canada Cataloguing in Publication data
available upon request to the publisher.

Visit the Penguin Group (Canada) website at **www.penguin.ca**
Special and corporate bulk purchase rates available;
please see **www.penguin.ca/corporatesales**
or call 1-800-810-3104, ext. 477 or 474

CONTENTS

Foreword

When we started this company, our daughters were four and two. Cleaning experiments in our home were part of their lives as they watched while Mom and Dad searched for the most efficient ways of organizing the MOLLY MAID cleaning process. Over the ensuing years they would witness professionally uniformed maid teams improving that process with videographers present for the new MOLLY MAID franchise training video.

Our home was where it all started and where it continued for several years, as we trained maids, supervisors, managers, and franchise owners alike. And when MOLLY MAID went international, Adrienne trained the new foreign owners in our cleaning process right in our home as well. They needed to start by learning our business from the customer's point of view.

Kimberly and Christine are now thirty-four and thirty-two and look upon MOLLY MAID as the sister they grew up with, ever-present and always growing with exciting new developments and accomplishments, just as they themselves have. Today Kimberly is a psychologist and Christine is a writer/producer in the film industry. MOLLY MAID is a multinational business with over six hundred franchises that clean approximately two million homes per year, one home at a time.

For nearly thirty years, each member of the international MOLLY MAID team has been part of the continual process of learning ways to improve the customer service experience. We've always said "The customer is part of our team" because we make a point of learning his or her needs, whether through a general discussion while we're cleaning their home or through customer feedback and focus groups.

We are proud to share the benefit of our experience in our customers' homes through this book. And we hope that it helps to create the mood that you strive for in your home as you serve the needs of each member of your family.

Adrienne and Chris Stringer,
MOLLY MAID founders

Introduction

MOLLY MAID has been cleaning houses for a long time—and we've perfected a strategic and efficient method for tackling all the chores that need to be done. Our method is sensible, environmentally preferable, and designed to keep your house clean and help make your life easier. (And you can't get neater than that!)

The company started in 1979 in Mississauga, Ontario—and it's a wonderful success story. As modern life was becoming busier and busier, our founders, Adrienne Stringer, a nurse, and her husband, Chris Stringer, saw a need for a home cleaning service to help people just like them. They decided to start one: MOLLY MAID would be a high-quality housecleaning service, delivered by a team of professionally trained and uniformed cleaners. Adrienne settled on recognizable pink and blue corporate colours, and Chris decided that staff would drive company-branded cars.

And the name? Here's where it gets really fun. MOLLY MAID was named after *The Unsinkable Molly Brown*, a popular movie in the 1960s starring Debbie Reynolds. What you may not know is that Molly (her real name was Margaret) Brown was born on July 18, 1867, and spent her life surviving obstacles to become a famous socialite and activist. The movie shows how she survived a flood that consumed her family when she was baby (hence the description "Unsinkable"). Then, as a poor teenager and young woman, Molly used her indomitable determination to rise above life's hurdles and accomplish her goals. She capped her extraordinary life by being a survivor of the sinking of the *Titanic*. Molly was on the British luxury passenger liner en route to New York from Southampton, England, when it hit an iceberg and sank on April 15, 1912. It was Molly's spirit and drive for accomplishment that the Stringers wanted for their new endeavour, and MOLLY MAID was born.

In England, Molly is a name for a trustworthy figure—and that fits the company to a T as well!

Just one year after the Stringers started MOLLY MAID, Jim MacKenzie, the current chairman and CEO of the company, and other individuals still active on its board of directors invested in the business because they believed the idea was a good one. And they were right. MOLLY MAID has grown exponentially in Canada and around the world. Today the company has hundreds of franchisees the world over.

Incidentally, the Stringers remain involved. Adrienne Stringer served as a franchise trainer for the first ten years, and she and Chris still attend company functions and actively support franchisees.

The success of MOLLY MAID, which is now the most recognized name in the cleaning industry, has always been associated with quality. Of course, from day one the company realized that the people who most represent it—the cleaning teams who visit our customers' homes regularly—would always be the most important part of the service. And they still are, as they provide unparalleled housecleaning to thousands of Canadians each and every day.

At the same time, MOLLY MAID has expanded not only across Canada but also into the United States, the United Kingdom, Japan, and Portugal. This year alone, the company will perform more than two million home cleanings!

And we want to do the very best job every time. MOLLY MAID has a comprehensive training program, and all our Home Service Professionals (HSPs) pass the test for their cleaning acumen and enthusiasm. This guarantees consistency across the company in cleaning methods and products. All staff follow the same practical, functional cleaning system in every room of the house—and that's what we want to share with you in this book.

Over the past several years we've been developing another important policy: we're moving away from traditional petroleum-based cleaning products where possible and using bio-based cleaning products instead. This comes from a commitment to protect the health and safety of our customers, our staff, and the environment.

There's one more part of our business that needs to be spotlighted: our customers. Everyone leads such a busy life these days, and keeping the house clean isn't always at the top of the priority list. But what's important to know is that cleaning, when done systematically and with care, is a way to give your life some order. Coming home to a clean home can help you get to all the other must-dos on your list without feeling frazzled or frustrated.

And that's where this book comes in. Our cleaning methods are simple, logical, and environmentally preferable—all the things you need them to be in this day and age. Alongside our step-by-step guide to cleaning each room in your house, we've included lots of tips, guidance from MOLLY MAID on cleaning specifics, and other great information to make the job easier, safer, and more effective.

Happy cleaning!

1
Getting Started

You can tell a lot about a person by taking a quick tour inside his or her home. Someone who has a clean and tidy home is usually pretty organized in other areas of life as well. Conversely, someone who has a messy home is often frazzled and running late.

If your day-to-day life is just one big whirlwind of demands and activities (or if keeping the house clean doesn't come naturally), don't worry. Getting organized about housecleaning is easy.

The first and most important step to a clean home is to declutter as best as you can. Cleaning in general is easier when there isn't a lot of "stuff" lying around. You may even have heard friends say that they've got to tidy up the house because MOLLY MAID is scheduled to clean the next day. Maybe you do that yourself. Of course that's because it's really tough to clean a house when dishes are strewn across the kitchen counter, shoes are scattered throughout the hallway, newspapers are in piles in various places in the living room, the beds aren't made, and clothing is all over the floor in the bedrooms … well, you get the picture.

Another thing about clutter is that it gets out of control in a really short time. One out-of-place item leads to another and another. Soon, cleaning is a massive chore, and the really important jobs—such as cleaning the kitchen counter, vacuuming the floor, and dusting the furniture—don't get done because you can't find those surfaces under all the stuff.

The way to manage this is to pick up as you go, always trying to return articles of clothing, newspapers and books, toys and pillows—and everything else that finds its way around the house—to their proper places. You may have to create homes and storage for these items. A good-sized wicker basket in the living room is a convenient place to put the morning newspaper when you're done reading it (or walk it straight out to the recycling bin)—and it helps keep the living room tidy. Give kids a big toy box and make it the place where all their toys live. Have a look in the front hall closet—is there room for another shelf above the coat rack? An extra shelf may be the perfect home for all the odds and ends scattered throughout that closet. Another good solution is to use storage bins that fit on the shelf. Give one to everyone in the house—and label each one by name. That way everyone takes responsibility for putting away hats, gloves, and so on. Consider having two storage bins per person: one for summer and one for winter. Depending on the season, store the bins in the hallway closet or in a storage area in the basement.

As you can see, tidying up is really all about habit and organization. Get into the habit of throwing junk mail into the recycling bin as you go through your mail rather than piling it on the dining room table. Pick up before you go to bed—walk through the living room and kitchen, collecting dirty dishes and garbage. Straighten out shoes and boots at the front door. Put hats and gloves in the front hall closet. Rearrange cushions on the couch.

In order to do this, everything has to have a home. Umbrellas go into an umbrella stand, bicycle helmets are hung up in the garage, and the dog's leash is looped on a hook by the door. In the bedroom and bathroom, perfume bottles and other small personal care items are organized in a decorative basket or on a tray.

If magazine and newspaper subscriptions are piling up, maybe it's time to re-evaluate everything you receive and cancel the ones you no longer read. If you're tired of receiving junk mail, put a sign on the mailbox that says junk mail isn't welcome.

It's also a good idea to take the time to declutter crammed drawers, cupboards, and closets regularly, and to put storage baskets and boxes in place. That way you'll know where to find what you're looking for!

Another way to help keep your home clean is to use mats inside and outside the front and back doors—a thick one for mud outside and another inside. Anyone who enters has the opportunity to wipe his or her feet twice before tramping through the house. Even better, make your home a "no shoes" zone. Lots of people do. Ask friends and family to kindly remove their shoes at the door. Your carpets will last longer and you really will save on cleaning. Keep a few pairs of inexpensive slippers and slipper socks at the door to lend to guests.

If you live in a home with several levels, develop a system where stuff that needs to go to another floor is left on the landing. And get everyone to pitch in and distribute stuff when going up or down the stairs.

All these habits will help—both with the cleaning you have to do and with the way you feel in general. Many people underestimate the importance of order in the home and how it helps you manage your emotions and life. When you open a drawer or a closet and everything is neat and orderly, there is unconscious relief. Compare that with how you feel when you're running on empty or rushing off to a yoga class or your daughter's piano lesson, and you're trying to find your yoga mat in a messy front hall closet or your daughter's songbook in a cluttered drawer. When closets are overfilled with stuff or you can't see anything for the jumble in the drawer, that's often the time you get pushed over the edge and lose it.

Here's another tip: Designate a place where you keep items you use every day such as keys and glasses so you won't waste time looking for them when you need them. For example, have a special hook or plaque for keys in the kitchen; keep glasses in a dresser drawer.

At the end of the day, while decluttering makes it so much easier to keep surfaces clean, it really does help reduce your stress as well.

So, starting now, put some cleaning policies in place for yourself. Stay on top of clutter as you go through your day, and set aside five or ten minutes before bed to tidy up. Commit to reorganizing drawers, closets, and other storage areas regularly. (As you're decluttering, you might also consider holding a garage sale to get rid of all the stuff you haven't used for a while or don't need anymore.) Make a commitment that every time you buy a new article of clothing because you need it, you throw out or give away something else.

Try to put things away more often at the time you're dealing with them. Hang up your coat when you get home. As you put groceries away, put carrying bags in the bag storage drawer. When you've finished reading a magazine, return it to the magazine rack.

Here are a few more organization tips.

* Recruit your children to help with a basic cleaning routine. Following a routine helps them develop good organizational habits and reduces the stress you feel when you have to constantly remind them to tidy their rooms.

* Buy a toy chest and put it at the end of your child's bed. Teach your kids that it's where toys and games are stored.

* For kids and adults, plastic bins or baskets on wheels that can be rolled into a closet or even under the bed are a great use of space. Store winter clothes in the bins during the summer, and vice versa.

* Always tidy up before any major clean. Take dirty dishes to the kitchen. Pick up toys. Collect newspapers and place them in the recycling bin.

* Look around at the surfaces in your home—maybe there's a better way to organize items. For example, instead of having an array of personal care items on the vanity counter, place them in a decorative basket or on a tray. Instead of leaving loaves of bread and other baked goods sitting in different spots on the kitchen counter, put them all in a bread basket.

* If you find it difficult to clean because of the large amount of time spent picking up and putting things away, establish a house rule that if you take something out, you put it away.

* Make another rule about items that haven't been used in a long time and may be just taking up space—donate these to a charitable organization, plan a yard sale, or set these items outside at the curb with a "Free" sign attached.

Motivate Yourself

If you're procrastinating about cleaning the house, here are some great ideas to light a fire.

* Declutter one room. There's nothing like cleaning out old garbage and long-dated items to give you a new lease on life—and on the prospect of cleaning the entire house. Getting rid of "old" stuff is a healthy thing to do. It's going to give you energy and a feeling of freedom. That may just be all the motivation you need to clean some more!

* Invite a friend or relative for dinner. This gives you a deadline and puts your home in a new light—you often start looking at your kitchen from a guest's point of view. Suddenly all the chores that need doing start screaming out at you! Make a date to see someone—and make a cleaning schedule too. Be sure to give yourself enough time to do the things that need doing.

* Buy something new for cleaning. It's nice to look at chores with a fresh perspective, and often a different cleaning product or gadget helps you do just that. Think about the cleaning jobs you've been putting off—and go shopping. Do your research and look for a cleaning product or gadget that will help get the job done.

* Make the house smell nice. Studies have suggested that scent can affect your mood … so what's your favourite uplifting scent? See if you can introduce it into the house and thereby motivate yourself to get cleaning. Consider an essential oil candle, for example: Invigorating essential oils include eucalyptus, rosemary, and vanilla. (At the same time, be sure that no one is allergic to the scent you like—that will definitely backfire.)

* Redesign a room. Changing the colour and decor of one room can often give your entire home a fresh feel. Maybe all you need is a lighter shade of paint on the walls, different covers on cushions, and a new piece of art? Putting the couch on another wall or changing the angle of a chair changes the look of a room, too—and can be inspirational. It might be all you need to start moving into other rooms and cleaning them as well.

Delegate Chores

Unless you live by yourself, there's really no reason why you should be doing all the cleaning. Most experts say that another aspect of being organized is taking charge of delegating chores to other people in the house and having a daily or weekly routine. Everyone contributes to the mess, so everyone should help keep the house clean, too. When it comes to your kids and their friends, these kinds of rules teach them about responsibility and teamwork. For adults, it's all about doing your part to help. It's just so much easier to clean when there's no clutter.

Here's a suggested list of daily chores to delegate.

* Make beds (everyone makes his or her own).

* Take out the garbage.

* Sort and wash the laundry.

* Fold and put away laundry.

* Clean counters in the kitchen.

* Pick up toys.

* Sweep the kitchen floor.

* Vacuum.

* Set the table.

* Clear the table.

Teach Your Kids to Help Out

It's never too early to start teaching children to help around the house. And kids don't see chores as chores when they're fun. Even a young child can help set the table or put dirty clothes in the hamper. As children get older, they should be given specific chores so that they know exactly what's expected. Remember, when you delegate chores and ask everyone in the family to help out, you're also teaching teamwork—and those skills will always come in handy.

Cleaning Essentials

MOLLY MAID has created this list of tools that will help you clean.

Attitude Go for it. You're going to have the cleanest house on the street!

Broom Bristles made of nylon catch dirt best, and an angled broom head can get into corners.

Body Wise

Look for a broom with a lightweight handle. It will help you avoid straining your shoulders while sweeping. At the same time, a longer broom handle is better for taller individuals.

Bucket Keep all your cleaning products in a bucket so that you'll always know where they are. (When you're using the bucket, be sure to use a cloth underneath to prevent damage to the floor in case contents spill over the side.)

Cleaning products MOLLY MAID recommends a core group of five bio-based cleaning products for the home. At times, and depending on how often the home is cleaned and what type of water is available (hard versus soft), additional products may also be required. When buying commercial cleaning products, look for the following environmentally preferable descriptions on the label: phosphate-free, low-phosphate, chlorine-free, non-toxic, and biodegradable. When using these products, always follow the manufacturer's instructions. For convenience, store these supplies in a plastic bucket or basket that can be carried from room to room. Here's the essentials list.

- glass cleaner
- all-purpose cleaner
- degreaser
- washroom cleaner
- disinfectant

Body Wise

You've probably heard that petroleum-based cleaning products should never be mixed together, and it's true—some in combination can create toxic fumes. Most bio-based cleaning products can be mixed—check the label.

Cloths Washable reusable cloths are recommended for cleaning. MOLLY MAID prefers microfibre cloths made from polyester, nylon, or a blend. These cloths are soft and keep their shape. They also require less product and are more effective for cleaning. They're highly absorbent—they hold on to water, bacteria, and other things you want to clean up. Also, you can just toss them into the washing machine when you're done cleaning. Don't put them into the dryer, though—simply hang to dry. For polishing and drying mirrors, windows, and pictures, for example, cloths should be lint-free and absorbent.

Duster An extendable duster is flexible, and can get at lower- and higher-hanging cobwebs and so on. (A feather duster is not an ideal choice because it really just moves the dust around.) Extendable dusters are available at local janitorial or hardware stores.

Garbage bags To lighten your load as you clean through the house, carry a small plastic garbage container (rather than a large green garbage bag that can fill up quickly and get awkward and heavy). Once the container is full, empty it into a green garbage bag in a central location.

Mops Look for a mop with a washable cloth head (flat-head mops are popular today) made of cotton or microfibre. For washing the floor, MOLLY MAID prefers a rag mop with a snap-on replaceable head. A larger-size mop head covers more ground and absorbs more liquid. A plastic wringer lever is convenient, and you won't have to get your hands wet.

Plastic scrubby tool A plastic, nylon, or wire scrubby is helpful when the surface you're cleaning needs scouring and rubbing in order to remove dirt.

Be sure the scrubby tool you purchase is gentle and safe to use on most surfaces.

Rubber gloves Protect skin from germs and cleaning agents by wearing rubber gloves when you clean. Check department and other stores for specialty gloves, such as latex-free gloves and gloves with a foam lining that absorbs inside wetness.

Scrub brush If you prefer a scrub brush (best for dimpled surfaces or really dirty surfaces), try the handle on for size before you buy it. A comfortable handle keeps your skin away from cleaners.

Special cleaning products For stain removal and special cleaning chores, MOLLY MAID will, at times, recommend the following: vinegar, lemon juice, baking soda, a bio-based dish soap, and a neutral cleaner (a general-purpose gentle scrub soap that's safe to use on any surface not normally harmed by water).

Squeegee A small squeegee in the shower and bathtub does a great job at removing excess water. Look for a squeegee with a durable rubber edge.

MOLLY MAID CLEANING PRODUCTS SHOPPING LIST

Essentials
* glass cleaner
* all-purpose cleaner
* degreaser
* washroom cleaner
* disinfectant

Extras
* vinegar
* lemon juice
* baking soda
* bio-based dish soap
* neutral cleaner

(Keep it in your shower, and ask everyone in the family to help clean the walls and shower doors with the squeegee after a shower.)

Toilet bowl caddy and soft brush For the toilet, MOLLY MAID recommends a brush with a long handle. A brush with non-absorbent nylon bristles repels germs and won't scratch the surface of the toilet. It's not essential, but one of these caddies for each bathroom in your house will make your life easier.

Toothbrush A toothbrush is imperative for tough-to-reach spots and crevices that your fingers can't get into, such as taps and drains in kitchens and bathrooms. A nylon bristle is recommended because it's non-absorbing. (An "orange peeler" gadget available in dollar stores and kitchen stores can also be a great help when cleaning narrow spaces such as window tracks. The gadget has a serrated V-point for scoring the peel. Wrap that end with a wet cloth to clean a dirty window track.)

Vacuum cleaner A good vacuum cleaner is a lifesaver. Make sure to read about your vacuum cleaner, and to use it properly for different floor surfaces. For example, there are usually attachments for special cleaning needs as well as an adjustment knob for different suctions depending on the surface. Change the bag as recommended for maximum suction. Change the filters as required. A smaller hand vacuum with a beater bar can simplify cleaning the stairs and upholstery.

SHOPPING FOR A VACUUM CLEANER?

You don't have to buy the most expensive vacuum cleaner. What you need is a machine that excels at the jobs you need done in your house. Here are some shopping considerations.

* Check the suction power, especially if you have deep-pile carpets. That's where you really need a strong machine.

* Match the vacuum to your mix of carpeting and floors. Uprights are great at cleaning carpets, but not necessarily floors. If you have lots of floor to clean, look for models with floor attachments. Also, make sure the

height can be set low enough and that the machine won't scratch flooring.

* Match the vacuum to the types of vacuuming chores you need done. Are there a lot of stairs and tight corners? Canisters are more versatile in terms of their cleaning ability.

* Do you need a HEPA (high-efficiency particulate air) filter? This is a sophisticated system that will remove a large percentage of pollens and mites from your home. While a HEPA filter system costs more, buying this type of machine makes sense if there are allergy sufferers in your household.

* Look for extras. Different brushes and nozzles, an attachment caddy, and indicators that show when the bag is full are helpful and make the job easier.

* Be sure you can assemble, disassemble, and store all those attachments without much fuss. And make sure they work.

* A warranty is always a good idea.

SELECTING THE PROPER VACUUM TOOL

Here's a guide to cleaning attachments.

Crevice tool This long, narrow tool may be used in tight spaces, corners, and along edges in places such as dresser drawers, upholstered furniture, stairs, and baseboards.

Dusting brush This attachment looks like a small brush and may be used for carved furniture, tabletops, books, lamps, light fixtures, venetian blinds, baseboards, shutters, and heat registers.

Furniture nozzle This small nozzle may be used for upholstered furniture, draperies, mattresses, clothing, and automobile interiors.

Hard floor tool This tool is usually wide with very short bristles and may be used for irregular hard-surface floors such as hardwood, brick, and slate.

The Clean Team

MOLLY MAID recommends the following core group of five bio-based cleaning products for the home. Unscented products are always preferable.

GLASS CLEANER

Tasks Use this product to clean windows, mirrors, and other shiny surfaces.

How to use Spray glass cleaner over the surface you're cleaning. Polish dry with a clean, lint-free cloth. To help you avoid leaving streaks on windows, use horizontal strokes to wash the window on one side and vertical strokes to wash the window on the other side. You'll know right away which side of the window has the streak.

Caution When cleaning a framed picture, always spray glass cleaner onto your cloth. Never spray glass cleaner directly onto a framed picture because it can seep under the frame and damage the picture. Wipe the top of the frame first, working down the sides and across the bottom.

ALL-PURPOSE CLEANER

Tasks This product is for cleaning tile and polished floors such as stone and terrazzo as well as most washable surfaces in the home.

How to use For washing floors, add from 1 capful to ¼ cup (50 mL) of concentrated all-purpose cleaner to a bucket of warm water and rinse your mop in the water. Always check usage directions on the label—if the product is not a concentrated formula, it usually comes in a spray bottle and can be used full strength. For other surfaces, spray onto the surface you are cleaning and wipe clean with a cloth.

DEGREASER

Tasks This product is recommended for removing greasy spots from kitchen surfaces, including stovetops, range hoods, and sinks.

How to use Spray and wipe tough jobs such as fingerprints on walls, countertops, and appliances that require degreasing. Allow the product to work for five minutes before cleaning heavily soiled areas.

Caution Since it is a degreaser, test it in an inconspicuous area before using to make sure there won't be colour fading.

WASHROOM CLEANER

Tasks This product is for cleaning all surfaces in the washroom, including toilets, sinks, tubs, tiles, and showers. It can remove hard water deposits, soap film, and body oils from bathroom fixtures, porcelain tiles, or fibreglass surfaces.

How to use Spray on and allow the product to remain on the surface to dissolve soils before cleaning. Allow it to sit for five minutes in hard water areas.

DISINFECTANT

Tasks Use this product to clean, disinfect, and deodorize walls, glazed porcelain, plastic surfaces, and any other hard, non-porous surface. It cleans and sanitizes surfaces such as toilets, doorknobs, telephones, and garbage cans.

How to use Spray on and let the disinfectant work on a surface for about ten minutes before wiping. To sanitize and clean, spray on a cloth and wipe the surface. No rinsing is required.

Bio-Based Products: The Smell of Clean

People tend to associate the smell of clean with the smell of harsh chemical cleaners. But MOLLY MAID as a company supports the policy of using unscented products where possible. Unscented products are not only better for the environment, but they can also help reduce health-related problems and symptoms in those who have chemical sensitivities and environmentally linked illnesses. Yet, since most of us have grown up with chemical cleaners and the way they smell, making the transition to unscented products isn't easy. MOLLY MAID has had to explain the decision to regular customers, giving the reasons why unscented products are preferable. "You just have to get used to the fact that clean doesn't have to have a strong smell," says a MOLLY MAID spokesperson. "When you come home from work to your clean house, it won't smell the way it would if petroleum-based cleaners had been used." Now there's a neutral smell—and that's pleasing to the nose and less harmful.

THE PRODUCTS ARE STILL EFFECTIVE

MOLLY MAID wouldn't use environmentally preferable products if they weren't effective. Still, it's important to know that these products work a little differently, often a little more slowly, and may change the order in which you clean. For example, bio-based products are not always "spray and wipe." It might be necessary to spray, leave for a few minutes while the product goes to work, then come back a few minutes later and wipe.

THE PRICE IS BECOMING RIGHT

There's another important point about bio-based cleaning products that we want to make, and it has to do with price. Many people assume that these products are more expensive than non-environmental cleaning products. Traditionally, that has been true. But start comparing prices more carefully. As more people choose to buy environmental products, the price points are shifting and becoming more similar to other cleaning products. Many large retailers now use bio-based products as loss leaders—they reduce their prices to get you into their stores. So read the flyers and compare prices. It's a great time to get on board and use bio-based cleaning products. Prices really are better than they were before.

MOLLY MAID Cleaning Basics

The MOLLY MAID method of cleaning is from "top to bottom and left to right" in whatever room you're cleaning. This is the quickest and most efficient way to clean, and we recommend it for any cleaning task: the whole house, a room, a bookshelf, or even a chair. Following this system means you'll always know what you've done and, therefore, make more efficient use of your time and do a more thorough clean.

The order in which you clean your house will depend on the layout and style of your home. MOLLY MAID likes to get the bathrooms done first, then the bedrooms and family rooms. The kitchen is usually last. If you have a two-storey home, head for the bathroom on the second floor and get that started. Proceed to the bedrooms on that floor. Then move to the living room and other family rooms. Finish with the kitchen. You'll have to bend the left-to-right rules a bit depending on the layout of your house, of course. Plus, there's only one of you cleaning! When cleaning a home, the MOLLY MAID team often divides tasks depending on whether they're wet or dry. So while one MOLLY MAID Home Service Professional does all the dusting and vacuuming, the other gets to work in the bathroom and kitchen, where there are lots of wet cleaning tasks.

The MOLLY MAID General Guide to Cleaning Every Room

Dust and clean everything in the room. Through no fault of your own, dust collects on surfaces and can lead to breathing issues and dull-looking surfaces. Start at the top of the room (the ceiling and walls) and work to the bottom (the floor and baseboards). In between, dust all the furniture, sills, shelves, blinds, and other decor. Always dust a room before you vacuum it. Any bits of dust and dirt will fall to the floor, where you'll suck them up with the vacuum cleaner.

Damp dusting is the best technique, working with a bucket of warm water and a microfibre cloth that traps dust particles. To dampen the cloth, hold it by a corner and lightly mist with clean water from a spray bottle or dunk it into the water and wring it out. The cloth should be just damp enough to pick up dust without leaving moisture streaks on the furniture.

Make sure to rinse the cloth frequently, and to carry a dry cloth for surfaces that require polishing after damp dusting. Also carry a polishing cloth to use with the glass cleaner for pictures and mirrors.

Begin in a room by using the extendable duster around the ceiling and light fixtures, into corners, and behind drapes and heavy furniture that can't be moved.

When dusting a piece of furniture, follow this procedure: First lift and dust each object; then dust the shelf or surface both underneath and behind. Start from the top of the unit and dust down to the bottom.

When dusting any large surface, bring the dust toward you with a side-to-side motion. If it's a wood surface, when you're done give the surface one last wipe along the grain of the wood to prevent streaking.

Shine and buff all shiny surfaces. A dry clean cloth will polish chrome to an eye-catching gleam. Use glass cleaner and a clean cloth to clean and shine mirrors, windows, and other shiny surfaces. (Consider having your windows cleaned professionally at least once a year. It's a good idea, of course, if you've got second-storey windows and you're averse to climbing ladders with the window cleaner and a cloth in your hands.) As described on page 14, avoid streaks by washing glass doors and windows with vertical strokes on one side and horizontal strokes on the other. That way, if there are any streaks, it's easy to tell which side they're on.

Sweep or vacuum all floors, carpets, rugs, and stairs. Vacuum cloth upholstery, too. Always sweep or vacuum kitchen and other floors first to collect crumbs and dirt before damp-mopping. Dust buildup is unsightly, and can trigger allergies and respiratory issues for your family and guests.

Change the vacuum bag as recommended by the manufacturer to maintain maximum suction.

If the vacuum has poor suction, you might have a blocked hose. To check, disconnect the hose and drop a quarter down its length. If the coin falls out, the hose is likely not the problem.

When vacuum cleaning, move the machine slowly over the carpet. Slow and steady vacuuming will gather more dirt and dust than several quick passes.

Be careful not to vacuum up anything that can damage the inside of the machine. For example, don't vacuum up open safety pins: They can damage the vacuum hose and be difficult to remove. Look underneath furniture before vacuuming so that the vacuum doesn't pick up small items such as toys, jewellery, or coins. Foil, and tinsel in particular, can damage the engine of the vacuum.

Only use a power head to vacuum carpeted areas. Never use a beater bar on hard surfaces. The beater bar can leave small marks on a hardwood floor.

A small hand vacuum with a beater bar is great for vacuuming upholstery and carpeted stair steps.

Body Wise

One way to lower the risk of spreading germs in your home is to clean all surfaces regularly with the appropriate cleaner.

Cleaning Schedules

We all lead such busy lives today that planning our time wisely is practically a necessity. Just as you write medical appointments, family gatherings, and other activities into your appointment book or calendar, it's important to schedule cleaning. When you keep track of different chores, you'll get them done and won't do them more than necessary.

How often should you clean? Obviously, some rooms need to be cleaned more than others—and that would be the high-traffic areas such as the front hallway, bathroom, and kitchen. It's easier and less time-consuming to clean these rooms on a regular basis so that you're maintaining them rather than allowing dirt to build up.

Once a week (or once every two weeks), it's important to clean the house from top to bottom. This depends on the size of your household, how busy everyone is, and even where you live (some areas of the country are dustier than others). Most people schedule a Cleaning Day, whether they hire a cleaning company such as MOLLY MAID to come in or they roll up their sleeves and get to work themselves. It's helpful to keep a list of the tasks you want to get done on this day. Sit down and think about it: If your home has two showers, for example, but the downstairs shower gets little traffic unless guests stay over … well, that shower doesn't need a thorough cleaning every Cleaning Day. Only you can determine which chores are done and how often.

There are also cleaning tasks that need doing only a few times a year—and that's where a Deep Clean schedule comes in. It acts as a guide to (and a reminder of) all the various cleaning tasks. By knowing what you plan on cleaning, and how often, you can develop a strategy that ensures nothing is overlooked. A good way to divide these tasks is to schedule them at the beginning of each new season.

The first item on the agenda, then, is the list of everyday cleaning activities.

EVERYDAY CLEAN

Here's a list of chores that everyone in the household can help with every day! If possible, post it where everyone will read it.

❏ Keep toilet bowl clean.

❏ Squeegee walls/shower door after shower.

❏ Make beds (everyone is responsible for his or her own).

❏ Put clothes and dirty laundry where they belong.

❏ Leave desk tidy.

❏ Pick up and return things to their place.

❏ Sort garbage and recycling as you create it.

❏ Wipe up all spills immediately.

❏ Put dishes into the dishwasher (or wash them by hand).

❏ Wipe out sinks.

❏ Wipe counters and the kitchen table.

❏ Change kitchen dishcloth.

❏ Sweep kitchen floor.

❏ Clean up after pets (yard).

❏ Clean off pets (when they come in).

CLEANING DAY
(WEEKLY OR BIMONTHLY)

Here's a list of chores to include on your weekly or bimonthly Cleaning Day.

GENERAL

- ❏ Dust ceilings and ceiling fans, light fixtures, wall coverings, windowsills, and furniture.
- ❏ Shake out and dust curtains and other window coverings.
- ❏ Vacuum or sweep bare floors.
- ❏ Vacuum carpets, rugs, and stairs.
- ❏ Clean surfaces, including doors and handles.
- ❏ Shake out/clean door mats and scatter rugs.
- ❏ Collect/empty trash.
- ❏ Wipe off all telephones.
- ❏ Wash floors.
- ❏ Clean and buff surfaces (mirrors, windows).

BATHROOM

- ❏ Change bath towels.
- ❏ Clean the toilet, sink, shower, mirrors, and floor.

KITCHEN

❑ Clean kitchen sink.

❑ Clean small and large kitchen appliances, inside and out.

❑ Clean compost bucket and garbage can.

❑ Clean pets' eating areas.

❑ Clean kitchen table.

BEDROOM

❑ Change the beds.

❑ Put away clean clothing.

❑ Put dirty clothing in the hamper.

❑ Do the laundry.

LIVING ROOM/FAMILY ROOM/DINING ROOM

❑ Clean lamps.

❑ Vacuum upholstery.

❑ Tidy surfaces.

❑ Clean mirrors and pictures.

❑ Dust and clean buffet.

❑ Clean dining room table.

HOME OFFICE

❏ Clean office equipment.

❏ Wipe down office chair.

❏ Dust books.

LAUNDRY ROOM

❏ Wipe appliances down in laundry room.

❏ Clean dryer lint trap.

OUTSIDE THE HOME

❏ Sweep/clean outside veranda and paths.

DEEP CLEAN
(ONE TO FOUR TIMES A YEAR)

Here's a list of chores that are important but can be done less frequently.

GENERAL

❏ Clean under and behind appliances.

❏ Clean under furniture.

❏ Shampoo carpets and upholstery.

❏ Clean closets, cupboards, and drawers.

❏ Pack and store seasonal clothing and gear.

❏ Clean curtains and other window coverings.

❏ Deep clean lighting fixtures.

❏ Clean and reverse ceiling fan blades.

❏ Polish wooden furniture.

❏ Polish frames of mirrors and pictures.

❏ Dust and clean books.

❏ Check batteries in smoke detectors (annual).

❏ Schedule professional maintenance of heating and cooling units (annual).

❏ Change furnace filter (as per manufacturer's recommendations).

❏ Clean fireplace/have fireplace professionally cleaned.

BATHROOM

❏ Launder shower curtain.

❏ Scrub bathtub mat.

KITCHEN

❏ Clean the oven, including racks.

❏ Degrease the stove's hood.

❏ Clean refrigerator condenser coils.

❏ Defrost the freezer.

❏ Deep clean small appliances.

❏ Clean out pantry and fridge.

BEDROOM

❏ Launder mattress covers and pillow protectors.

❏ Launder or replace pillows.

❏ Turn the mattress.

❏ Clean blankets, duvets, and pillows.

HOME OFFICE

❏ Have computer professionally serviced.

OUTSIDE THE HOME

❑ Clean windows inside and out (check weather stripping and seals).

❑ Clean exterior doors.

❑ Clean grills and patio furniture (summer and fall).

❑ Clean gutters (fall and spring).

❑ Inspect garages, basements, lofts, and sheds.

2
Bathroom

In the late nineteenth century, "bath days" were a big production in most households. The bathtub—a metal-lined wooden container—was brought into the kitchen for the weekly event. The tub was filled with hot water from the stove, and everyone in the family who needed a good scrubbing took a turn. And the first few family members into the tub were the luckiest, because by the time the last bathers had their turns, the water was well used.

Thank goodness bathrooms and plumbing systems have evolved. During the second half of the nineteenth century, enamelled cast-iron baths started to appear in wealthier homes. Then, around the turn of the century, John M. Kohler (of the bathroom fixture company) sensed a business opportunity and modified a combination horse trough/hog scaler by putting enamel on it and adding legs. Just imagine: The modern-day bathtub was a *horse trough* in years gone by.

Today's bathroom is a splendid combination of function and comfort. While it may be like Grand Central Station during the morning rush hour, the bathroom must also transform into a place where you can escape from the world … by dimming the lights and climbing into a soaker tub filled with warm water and tiny bubbles.

Of course, for hygienic purposes, the bathroom needs to be clean—and cleaned more regularly than any other room in the house.

EVERYDAY CLEAN

It's easier and less time-consuming to clean a bathroom if you do it on a regular basis. The goal is to maintain the room's cleanliness instead of letting mildew, soap scum, and other dirt get out of hand. Here are some tips for daily bathroom cleaning.

* Keep a small window squeegee in the shower, and encourage everyone to use it after showers. Removing water and soap from the walls and shower door after every use slows down the formation of water spots.

* Keep a microfibre cloth under the sink, and wipe out the sink every time you use it.

* Wipe tap and toilet handles every day. They come into contact regularly with hands contaminated after using the toilet.

* Keep a handheld vacuum near the bathroom to vacuum the floor every day.

* Avoid filling the bathroom with clutter. Store products and small appliances off the counter and in their place. Arrange small bottles and containers in a decorative basket or tray. Put hair dryers and other bulky items in bins or baskets.

* Regularly go through products and throw out (or give away) the ones you never use.

* Sponges, loofahs, and plastic ducks and other bath toys can develop mildew. Shake off excess water—after you've turned off the shower or as the tub drains. Allow to dry. Replace them periodically.

* Close the shower curtain after every use—spreading it out (rather than pushing it together) will inhibit mildew.

* Keep a wastebasket under the sink and out of sight. If you can't do that, always use a clean plastic liner bag in the wastebasket. Sprinkle a little baking soda into the bag to help avoid odours.

* To prevent hair clogs in the tub or shower drain, use a drain protector (available at a plumbing supply store or a hardware, department, or dollar store) to catch hair.

* Keep the toilet brush next to the toilet—and remind everyone to help keep the toilet bowl spotless.

* Consider buying a high-efficiency toilet with good flushing power. It really does help keep the bowl clean.

* Keep matches, potpourri, scented candles, and other essential oil products in the room for freshness. But always keep matches out of children's reach.

* When light bulbs are cool, dab perfume or essential oil on them to scent the room when the bulbs heat up.

* Make sure there's a hamper for dirty laundry or towels.

* Change towels and facecloths regularly.

CLEANING DAY

Clean bathrooms from top to bottom and left to right. Here's a general bathroom cleaning checklist, followed by a more thorough guide to cleaning the different areas of the bathroom.

❏ Clean all shelves, fixtures, and items on vanity.

❏ Damp wipe cabinet fronts.

❏ Clean the shower, tub, and sink inside and out.

❏ Clean, dry, and shine all mirrors, chrome, and tile.

❏ Wash windows and tracks as needed.

❏ Scrub the toilet, including the bowl, seat, lid, tank, and base.

❏ Empty the garbage.

❏ Vacuum and wash the floor.

GETTING STARTED

"Think about how delightful it is to check into a hotel and use the shiny clean bathroom. Your bathroom at home should always be that clean."

* Put dirty towels into the hamper.

* Remove the wastebasket, scale, and bath rugs. Empty the basket, dust off the scale, and put these and the rugs into the hallway. Shake out or vacuum the rugs later.

* Flush the toilet and squirt washroom cleaner inside the bowl and under the rim. Let the product work while you clean other areas of the bathroom.

* Fill the sink with hot water and a small amount of cleaner. Place any soap dishes and glasses into the sink to soak.

* Use an extendable duster to dust ceiling area and walls. Dust into the corners, the exhaust fan, and light fixtures. Make sure the light is off, however, because light bulbs get pretty hot. (And remember, a hot light bulb will shatter when wiped with a damp cloth.)

* Use a damp cloth to wipe down door frames and mouldings, looking for fingerprints, especially around switchplates. If desired, use disinfectant on switchplates and doorknobs.

* Rinse your cloth often!

* Dust the toilet paper holder.

* Continue dusting around the room, including pictures, shelves, and towel bars.

* Fold and neatly arrange other towels.

* Wipe the baseboards.

Body Wise

Wear rubber-soled shoes when you clean the bathroom in order to protect yourself from slipping and falling. Non-slip shelf liner or a non-slip pad for under carpets can also help. Use them inside and outside the shower stall and bathtub to create a surface that provides grip. Ask about these products in department and home supply stores.

TUB AND TILE AREA

"Taking a bath or shower should be a wonderful experience ... not one where you're discovering mildew in different places ..."

* Always start by removing the slip mat in the bathtub, if there is one.

* Remove everything from around the tub, including bottles of shampoo, soap, conditioner, and so on.

* Fill the bucket with hot water. Rinse out a cloth and wring it out.

* Clean the tiles or walls of the bathtub/shower by spraying with washroom cleaner and letting it sit for a few minutes—this will give it time to work. If tiles go up to the ceiling, use a rag mop with a snap-on replaceable mop head or a flat-head mop with a microfibre cloth pad to reach up high. Whatever you do, don't stand on the ledge of the tub.

* Scrub walls from top to bottom using a side-to-side motion and overlapping as you move down.

* Use the scrub brush if necessary for hard-to-clean grout and tile surfaces.

* Use the toothbrush to reach areas around the soap holder, taps, faucets, and the space between the tiles, tub, and drain as well as the corners of the tub where products usually sit.

* Clean the showerhead and taps.

* Once you've removed all the soap scum and water stains, use a wet cloth or cup to rinse.

* Clean the inside and outside of shower doors with washroom cleaner.

* Clean the slip mat, which tends to build up soap scum. You might need to soak it. Be sure to turn it over and clean any slimy buildup on the bottom.

* Wet the sides and bottom of the tub, then apply washroom cleaner. If necessary, leave it to work for a few minutes.

* Clean around the tub ledge as if you're cleaning a shelf. Wipe each item you removed earlier, then replace.

* Wipe the sides and bottom of the tub.

* Use a toothbrush to clean the overflow drain and drain hood.

* Rinse thoroughly. Dry and shine the inside of the tub with a dry cloth.

* Polish all chrome surfaces with a dry cloth.

Body Wise

Never stand on the edge of the bathtub and/or hang on to the shower bar to keep your balance. And don't stand outside the tub and lean in to clean—that's hard on your back. Step slowly into the tub instead: Its surface might be slippery, and you risk skidding or falling. It's always a good idea to take your time when you're cleaning so that you're conscious of how you're moving your body.

Q: Are there any cleaning shortcuts for the tub that you can recommend?

MM: Run the shower on hot for a few minutes—steam makes it easier to clean the tiles. Or, if possible, schedule cleaning for after someone has taken a shower—when tiles are still damp from the shower.

Q: I've just moved into a house that hadn't been cleaned properly for years. The shower door is caked with soap scum. What's the best way to get rid of it?

MM: Try the washroom cleaner a few times and be sure to give it time to work. Scrub the surface from top to bottom with a scrub brush.

Q: There's lime scale on my shower door. How do I get rid of that?

MM: You may need to use a special lime-scale-remover product—ask at a home supply or hardware store. Finish by spraying glass cleaner onto the door and wiping.

Q: The door runners and tracks of the shower door are disgusting. How do I get rid of the grunge?

MM: Saturate a low-grade steel-wool pad or a toothbrush with washroom cleaner and scrub inside and outside the door runners from left to right. Go over the areas with a wet cloth. Dry with a clean cloth.

Q: The plastic shower curtain liner has mildew on it. How can I get that off?

MM: Just so you know, this isn't unusual. Mildew on shower curtains can build up sometimes overnight. To remove, make a paste of baking soda and water (three parts baking soda to one part water), put it on a cloth, and rub over the mildew until it comes off. Easier still, take the curtain down and wash it in the washing machine. Be sure to wash it with a few towels so the curtain liner doesn't scrunch up in the wash. Another consideration: How old is the liner? It might just be time to dispose of it and get a new one.

ACRYLIC TUBS AND SHOWERS

Clean acrylic tubs and showers with a soft cloth and warm soapy water. DON'T use the following cleaners in acrylic tubs and showers:

* cleaners with a powdery base—they may scratch the surface
* cleaners with an acidic base (any harder surface cleaners and descalers; also vinegar and lemon, which are mild acidic cleaners)—they may damage the surface
* undiluted strong detergents formulated for use on tile or porcelain enamel surfaces or abrasive cleaning products—again, these may damage the surface

---

SINK AREA

"One of my hang-ups is toothpaste splatters on the mirror—you really want to remove those."

* Clean the vanity, working from top to bottom and left to right.
* Tidy the counter and sink area. Unplug any small appliances such as a curling iron, hair dryer, and razor. Return items such as tweezers, hair brush, and face cream to their storage place.
* Fill the sink with warm water and add a little washroom cleaner. Wash the soap dish and any bathroom cups.
* Wash the countertop. Clean items on the countertop and replace them. Most containers on the sink (whether they're plastic, stainless steel, or porcelain) can be cleaned with a cloth dampened with washroom cleaner and water.

* Clean the backsplash and wall around the counter and the counter around the sink. Wipe drawers and cupboard fronts, paying particular attention to fingerprints and dust that collects around the mouldings and ledges. Wipe handles.

Body Wise

Always clean the drinking glass in the bathroom on Cleaning Day. But remind everyone in the family to rinse out the glass after they use it, too!

* Drain the sink. Wipe around the taps, faucet, and drain. Use a grout brush to clean around the base of and under the taps and along the faucet and drain.

* Clean drains and overflow holes with a cloth or cotton swab moistened with washroom cleaner or an orange peeler gadget.

* Don't forget to clean the stopper, too.

* Spray the sink, wipe sides and bottom, rinse, and shine.

* Dry and polish the sink, taps, and faucet with glass cleaner.

* Clean the mirror with a polishing cloth and glass cleaner, and be sure to check for streaks. Wipe in a circular motion, from the outside of the mirror in and from top to bottom.

* Change towels at least once a week, more often if someone in the family is sick.

Q: No matter how often I clean the soap dish, it gets scummy. Any ideas?

MM: After cleaning the soap dish with washroom cleaner, rub a bit of bath oil on the surface. That way the soap can't stick to it.

Q: How do I remove all the toothpaste splatters from the mirror?

MM: Congratulate your family members for being so vigorous about brushing their teeth, but ask them to be more careful. Then, the honest answer is elbow grease. Rub any toothpaste and water spots (as well as hairspray residue and other spots) with a cloth wet with hot water. The water—and elbow grease—should be enough to get them off.

CLEAR THE DRAIN

To clean drains and clear minor blockages in the bathroom drain, tip a handful of baking soda down the pipe, followed by ½ cup (125 mL) of vinegar. Leave for half an hour and flush with boiling water.

TOILET

"Cleaning the toilet has got to be the most despised job on the list. But it's a joy when it's done!"

* Lift the lid and spray with washroom cleaner. Spray everywhere, including under the rim. Let it sit.
* Wipe the top, sides, and front of the tank.
* Clean the lid, seat, ledge, and hinges behind seat. Clean the front of the toilet.
* Lift the seat and wipe underneath the rim where dirt always collects and around water holes and down the sides.
* Use the toilet brush to clean the inside of the toilet bowl.
* Wipe and replace the toilet brush holder.
* Close and flush the toilet.

* Clean the outside of the bowl, working your way down to the floor. Clean carefully around the base. Wipe under the tank and the water intake valve. A grout brush may help to clean around the hinges, floor bolts, and base of the toilet on floor.

* Don't forget to clean the handle of the toilet with soapy water or disinfectant—people rarely wash their hands before they flush.

* Clean a bidet in the same way as a toilet, paying attention to the rim. Dry the bowl and rim with a dry cloth when you're done.

* Once you're finished these tasks, put the used cloth aside for the laundry.

Q: I have hard-water stains in the toilet bowl. How do I get those off?

MM: Try rubbing the stains with a natural pumice stone, which you can buy at hardware stores. Be sure to keep the stone moist to avoid scratching.

CLOSE THE TOILET LID, THEN FLUSH

You don't often think about things like this, but flushing the toilet can cause particles to splash out of the toilet bowl and land on your skin or reach even farther to surfaces such as the bathroom sink. Always close the lid before flushing (be sure to teach your kids to do this too!) and clean the toilet bowl on a weekly basis.

Celebrate World Toilet Day

In 2001, November 19 was declared World Toilet Day by fifteen toilet associations around the world. There have been many World Toilet Summits and other regional conferences to coordinate and promote toilet and sanitation conditions worldwide. Toilet associations promote clean toilets and lobby for better equality (more facilities for women), more accessibility and special provisions (for the disabled and mothers with babies), and more toilets everywhere. The World Toilet Organization now has 151 member organizations in fifty-three countries.

FLOOR

"I don't care what you say—a clean and shiny floor is the finishing touch in a bathroom. Replace the mats and garbage container, and you're done."

* Vacuum or sweep the bathroom floor, starting in the corner farthest from the door.

* Soak a cloth in the bucket filled with hot water and all-purpose cleaner and wring out. Wipe the baseboards and into the corners.

* Mop or wash the floor, and be sure to rinse the mop or cloth often.

Body Wise

Kneeling on the hard floor is tough on your knees. Use a rolled-up towel or wear a pair of kneepads.

* If there are streaks, dry them with a clean cloth.

* While the floor dries, clean the garbage container and shake out or vacuum the bath rugs. Replace the garbage container and rugs. Never put a rubber-backed rug on a wet floor. The rubber will discolour the floor, and it can even stick to the floor, which could leave a mess next time you pull it up.

* Give the bathroom one last look. Make sure there are no stray hairs any-where, the mirror is streak-free, and all chrome is shining!

QUICK CLEAN

SURPRISE! COMPANY IS COMING AND WILL BE HERE IN TEN MINUTES

No doubt someone is going to use the bathroom when guests visit. So make sure to clean your guest bathroom (and don't worry about any other bathrooms in the house).

* Remove any towels (put them into the hamper) and put out fresh hand towels.

* If possible, close the shower curtain or spray visible shower walls with washroom cleaner and water and run a dry squeegee down the walls.

* Wipe down the counter and sink.

* Clean the mirror with glass cleaner and clean and shine the faucet and taps.

* Swab a toilet brush around the bowl. Wipe the toilet seat and the outer rim.

* Shake out the bath rugs.

* Sweep or vacuum the floor and wipe any spots off the floor.

* Wipe any fingerprints off the switchplate and door.

* Move housecoats from the back of the door to your bedroom.

* Make sure there's soap out for washing hands. Put out a hand moisturizer too.

* Make sure there are extra rolls of toilet paper—and that they're easy to spot.

* Light an essential oil scented candle (provided no one is allergic to the scent).

DEEP CLEAN

"You can't clean the shower curtain every day …
but when you do get around to it, a clean
curtain can make all the difference in the
world!"

* Body oils combined with soap scum can really make shower curtains look disgusting. Wash the curtain periodically, whether it's vinyl or cloth. How to do it: Take down the curtain and liner and remove the rings. Put them into the washing machine with detergent or 1 cup (250 mL) of baking soda. Wash in a complete cycle with warm water (or follow the instructions for washing on the curtain). Make sure to wash it with a few towels so that the curtains don't scrunch up in the wash. If the curtain is vinyl, remove it before the spin cycle and hang to dry. Cloth curtains can be tumbled dry on low or can be hung up wet.

* If the bath is also a shower, wash the slip mat on both sides with hot soapy water and a soft brush or cloth. This is a weekly and deep clean chore, since these mats can get grungy.

* To clean venetian blinds, line the tub with an old sheet or towel and take down the venetian blinds from the window. Fill the bathtub with water to cover, then soak the blinds in the bathtub in a full-strength all-purpose cleaning solution (one capful to a bucket of water). The sheet or towel will prevent scratches.

* Clean out the medicine cabinet. Remove and place the contents in an empty sink or container. Mist the walls and shelves with all-purpose cleaner and wipe them with a cloth. Rinse and wring the cloth out, and repeat. Clean each item before you put it back into the medicine

cabinet. If medication is past its expiry date, take it to your local pharmacy for proper disposal.

* Wipe down mouldings.

* Clean the fan and fan blades thoroughly with the brush attachment on the vacuum. You might need a ladder to reach the fan, so be sure to do this safely. Use a damp cloth to clean dust and dirt that has accumulated on the vent.

* If there's a window, remove the panes from the frame, if you can, and wash the different surfaces.

* To keep the showerhead in the best working condition, clean it periodically. Unscrew and remove the nozzle. Pour vinegar into a bowl and immerse the head. Soak the head overnight to dissolve stains. In the morning, scrub off slime with a toothbrush and water. Poke out hardened mineral deposits stuck in the perforations. Rinse and reconnect.

Bathroom Cleaning Schedule Checklist

EVERYDAY CLEAN

- ❑ Declutter.

- ❑ Wipe out sink.

- ❑ Wipe tap handles and faucet.

- ❑ Fold up towels.

- ❑ Keep toilet bowl clean.

- ❑ Squeegee walls/shower door after showers.

CLEANING DAY

- ❑ Shake out/clean bath rugs.

- ❑ Dust ceiling, windowsills, and baseboards.

- ❑ Clean vanity.

- ❑ Wipe walls, doors.

- ❑ Clean the toilet.

- ❑ Clean and polish sink, shower, and tub.

- ❑ Clean, dry, and shine all mirrors, chrome, and tile.

- ❑ Collect/empty trash.

- ❏ Change bath towels.

- ❏ Vacuum/sweep floor.

- ❏ Wash floor.

DEEP CLEAN

- ❏ Launder bath rugs.

- ❏ Clean out cupboards and drawers.

- ❏ Clean the fan.

- ❏ Clean the medicine chest.

- ❏ Wash shower curtain and liner.

- ❏ Wash windows and window coverings.

- ❏ Deep clean lighting fixtures.

- ❏ Scrub bathtub slip mat.

3

Kitchen

Food historians tell us that in days of old, the kitchen wasn't just the centre of the house, it was the entire house. The "house," in fact, consisted of one room with a heat source where everyone cooked, slept, and ate. Things have changed, obviously, and today the kitchen is a room designed with cooking, convenience, and lifestyle in mind, with a wide range of appliances that have evolved for function and style.

Although the kitchen's main function is, of course, food storage and preparation, it remains the heart of a home. If it's large enough to have a dining area—and today many are—kids often do their homework at the table so that parents can keep an eye on them. Washer/dryer combinations are increasingly located in the kitchen, often hidden away in a large closet or tucked around a corner—a very convenient arrangement, since it means you're not trucking up and down the basement stairs. Many people have also found a place for a small television in the kitchen so that they can watch the news or their favourite show while they prepare a meal. And who hasn't sat in the kitchen in the middle of the night with a glass of water or a mug of warm milk and a cookie?

The kitchen is also often the centre of a party. Everyone knows that when there's a gathering, many people tend to gravitate toward the kitchen. The room is warm, comfortable, and comforting because it's where all the delicious food aromas begin! As a popular kitchen trivet says, *No matter where you serve your guests, it seems they'll like your kitchen best.* And it's still true to this day.

So, with all this activity, the kitchen needs to be clean. And therein lies one of the biggest challenges, since the kitchen is arguably the highest-traffic room in the house, with people trudging through with their shoes on, not to mention the garbage and compost containers under the sink and the family pet's water and food bowls on the floor by the door.

So how do you keep the kitchen clean?

First and foremost, it's important to try to keep things clean and tidy every time you use the kitchen. It's no fun to come home to dirty dishes on counters, old food sitting in pots and pans, and dust bunnies and dirt from outside noticeable on the floor. While it's not always possible to keep the kitchen clean as you use it, when the intention is there, you're far more likely to try.

EVERYDAY CLEAN

Here are some ways to keep your kitchen hygienic and tidy between Cleaning Day cleans. Be sure to share these ideas with everyone in the family.

* Try to remove as much of the unnecessary clutter from surfaces as possible.

* Discard or store appliances and gadgets you don't use anymore.

* Wipe the stove every time you use it.

* Wipe up spills and splatters every time you cook. And try to wipe them immediately—because this is when they're easiest to clean. Once a spill has dried and hardened, it'll be more difficult to remove.

* Be especially vigilant when spills are foods high in sugar, such as milk and tomato-based foods—these may etch or damage a surface. Wipe up these spills immediately with a dry cloth.

* When the meal is over, clean off plates and other dishes and put them into the dishwasher.

* Soaking dishes in the sink is unnecessary—and creates unnecessary clutter—unless you're soaking off stuck-on food. As a general rule, wash dishes and pots and pans right away or put them directly into the dishwasher.

* Put away any food on the counter.

* Recycle empty containers and other food packaging.

* Use a garbage can with a lid. Clean up any spills.

* When the garbage is full or it smells, tie up the bag and put it into the garbage can outside. Put a new bag into the can. To save time, leave a bunch of folded bags in the bottom of the garbage can. (Do the same in the compost container if you keep one in the kitchen.)

* Tie up bags of compost material before they get too full and put them outside, in either your outdoor compost pile or the larger compost container that the municipality picks up during the week.

* When cupboards overflow with items, clean them out and rearrange them so that they're neat and tidy.

* Wipe surfaces before and after food preparation. Be sure to rinse the dishcloth you use for wiping surfaces often and to change it every day. Pull out a clean dishcloth every morning and put the dirty cloth into the laundry at the end of the day.

* Depending on how much your use dish towels, change them every few days.

* Keep an essential oil scented candle on the counter—sometimes you don't even have to light it to get a whiff of the fragrance and a little jolt of feeling good. Or light it and take a tea break.

* Suspend small appliances such as a radio or microwave under cupboards if possible. That way, you preserve counter space and keep the area clutter-free.

* Have two chopping boards—one for raw meat, another for vegetables.

* Keep the sink wiped out, and always empty and clean the drain of old food and other garbage.

* Keep an eye on best-before dates and get rid of food in the cupboard and fridge that is past its date.

* Keep the inside of your fridge clean, wiping up spills with a damp cloth as soon as they occur. The fridge will look and smell better, and will also work most efficiently this way.

* Consider finding another spot for your pet's dishes and meals. If you do leave the dishes in the kitchen, be sure to clean them out every day. Old food attracts bugs and vermin.

* Use mats by doors so that people can either remove their shoes or wipe them off.

* Review the clippings, pictures, and so on that you've put on your fridge door—is there anything you can recycle or throw away?

* Hang up a chalkboard or bulletin board and create a "Need to Buy" list. Invite everyone in the family to add to the list.

* Have a family rule: Anyone who brings anything to the kitchen table (a book, a puzzle, math homework) has to put it away when he or she is finished.

* Establish a closet or cupboard for cleaning tools such as brooms and mops—and use it. (Leaving the broom leaning in a corner creates clutter.)

* Avoid using metal scouring pads, steel wool, abrasives, and powdered cleaning products on kitchen surfaces such as stainless steel, ceramic, porcelain enamel, marble, limestone, and so on. These products can scratch and permanently damage different surfaces.

* Avoid using vinegar, lemon juice, or other acidic cleaners on marble and limestone surfaces.

GERMS IN THE GARBAGE

When you change your garbage bag, you could be spreading bacteria from the bag to your garbage can. Avoid this by cleaning the garbage can regularly with disinfectant and water and making sure that it's dry before putting in a new bag. Also, always wash your hands after touching a dirty garbage bag!

CLEANING DAY

Most people give their homes a good cleaning once a week or once every two weeks. For Cleaning Day, MOLLY MAID recommends cleaning each room from left to right—so that you don't forget what needs doing. Here's a general kitchen cleaning checklist, followed by a more thorough guide to cleaning the different areas in the kitchen.

❏ Clean, dry, and shine all appliance surfaces, range hood, and sink.

❏ Clean stove drip pans and burner grates.

❏ Use a degreaser product to wash countertops.

❏ Damp wipe cupboard fronts, table, and chairs.

❏ Clean the microwave oven inside and out, including the turntable.

❏ Clean the fridge, wiping shelves and the door rim, where mould often develops.

❏ Check if windows and other glass surfaces in the kitchen need to be washed.

❏ Sweep and wash the floor.

❏ Launder kitchen dishcloths regularly. Wash separately in hot water.

❏ Dish towels can easily become contaminated with salmonella. Throw your dish towel in the washing machine immediately after cooking meat or chicken. The hot water cycle is best to avoid transferring germs onto other items. Always wash dish towels and kitchen cloths separately from bath towels … too many germs.

COUNTER AREA

"Counter space shouldn't be a luxury. And when the counters are messy, the whole kitchen looks bad."

* Start by tidying dirty dishes left on counters. Clear the workspace around the sink, and put dirty dishes into the dishwasher (or do the dishes if you don't have one). Start from the left side of the kitchen counter area, and use a damp cloth to clean around the room.

* Fill the sink with hot water and add a small amount of degreaser or dish-washing liquid. Depending on the type of stove you have, remove burner rings and drip pans and put them into the sink to soak. Remove the control knobs of the stove if possible and put those into the sink, too. Soak the dish rack if you have one (whether it's plastic or stainless steel) to loosen food particles. Scrub them off with a toothbrush and dry with a clean cloth.

* Use an extendable static duster to dust around the ceiling of the kitchen and the eating area, including the ceiling light fixtures, behind any curtains, and in corners. Dust away any cobwebs.

* Wash cupboard fronts, wiping from top to bottom. Make sure to clean any fingerprints and smudges on doors, door handles, and ledges. Look underneath upper cupboards for spots and grease marks.

* Clean countertops with a damp cloth and mild dishwashing soap. Countertops are made of different materials, including marble, granite, solid surface synthetics, tile, and laminate. And many of these surfaces

are easily scratched, so don't use an abrasive cleaner, scrubby, or the rough surface of a dual-sided sponge.

* Lift and move any small appliances away from the wall on the counter-tops (avoid sliding them because they may scratch the surface). Clean and shine all small appliances. Be sure to remove food stains and fin-gerprints. And don't forget to empty the crumb tray in the toaster.

* Wash the wall and backsplash, and make sure to tackle the dust and grease on top of the backsplash ledge.

* Carefully replace all the small appliances.

* Rinse the cloth often.

Q: My husband just installed a new ceramic tile counter. How can I protect it and keep it looking new?

MM: Good question. There are several ways to make your counters last a long time. First, let's hope he used a medium- to dark-coloured grout, because those colours hide stains. Always line counters with parchment paper when cooking with citrus foods such as lemons or oranges—these foods contain acids that can discolour the countertop. And always use trivets or pot holders for hot pots so that you don't burn the surface.

Q: What's the best way to clean my chopping block?

MM: Use soap and water, then rinse well. For tough stains, squeeze some lemon juice on the spot and let it sit for ten minutes. Then wipe. Rubbing a slice of lemon across a chopping block disinfects the surface, and it smells nice too!

> **ROOM FRESHENERS THAT WORK IN THE KITCHEN**
> * Prevent cooking odours by simmering vinegar—1 tablespoon (15 mL) in 1 cup (250 mL) of water—on the stove while cooking.
> * To remove strong smells such as fish and onion from utensils and cutting boards, wipe with vinegar and wash in soapy water.
> * Keep fresh coffee grounds in a bowl on the counter.
> * Grind up a slice of lemon in the garbage disposal if you have one.
> * Simmer water and cinnamon or other spices on the stove.

APPLIANCES

"Clean and shiny appliances make you feel good … and sometimes it's as simple as wiping off the fingerprints."

The Dishwasher

"The dishwasher does the dishes for you, but it's also a great place to hide dirty dishes when unexpected company is on its way and you need to tidy up fast."

* Wash the front of the dishwasher. Open the door and clean any food stains on the inside door and lips.

* If the door of the dishwasher is plastic, wipe it with a cloth and all-purpose cleaner. Dry with a damp cloth. If it's a stainless steel door, dampen a cloth with water and a little dish detergent. Always wipe with the grain.

* Pull out racks and wipe down the inside with a wet cloth. Be sure to scrub the racks' wheels. You might need a toothbrush to get at the mechanism.

Q: Can I put non-stick cookware in the dishwasher?

MM: Many items are dishwasher-safe, but it's always best to play it safe and check with the manufacturer of the cookware for cleaning instructions.

Q: How do I remove cooked-on food from non-stick cookware?

MM: Easy. Fill the cookware with water. Add ½ cup (125 mL) of vinegar and bring to a boil. Let it cool. The residue should now be easy to remove.

Q: My dishwasher smells inside. How can I get rid of the smell?

MM: Here's a great solution: Use vinegar instead of the rinse-aid product—just pour vinegar into the rinse-aid compartment. Do this as often as required.

CLEANING STAINLESS STEEL

Stainless steel appliances have been all the rage in kitchens for several years now. But this surface is easily scratched. Always clean with warm water, a soft cloth, and a mild non-abrasive cleaner. MOLLY MAID uses a gentle washroom (and fixture) cleaner for stainless steel. Don't use anything rough (such as the rough side of a two-sided sponge), and be especially careful if you wear rings or bracelets. Remove your jewellery or wear rubber gloves. And dry stainless steel quickly, because it spots and streaks easily. Always wipe in the direction of the grain.

Microwave

"The microwave often saves the day when you're home late from work and you need dinner. But always cover food that you're warming up. If you overcook the food, you may end up with food particles all over the inside of the microwave!"

* Open the door and clean the inner lip and the window inside and out. Keep in mind that many doors are made of soft plastic, so use just a damp cloth to clean this surface. If it's a stainless steel door, dampen a cloth with water and non-abrasive cleaner. Always wipe with the grain.

* Remove the glass shelf and wash it in the sink. Clean the inside of the microwave.

* To soften cooked-on splatters inside, fill a cup with water, place it in the centre of the microwave, and turn it on high for three minutes. The steam will loosen any baked-on food so that it can be wiped clean. (And take care that the water doesn't boil over the cup and burn your hand.)

* Clean under the microwave by using the handle of the duster to push a cleaning cloth under the cabinet edge.

* Wipe the exterior with a cloth sprayed with all-purpose cleaner. For stainless steel machines, dip a cloth in water and dishwashing liquid, wring it out, and wipe with the grain.

Q: The microwave still smells like the popcorn my kids made in it a week ago. How can I remove the smell?

MM: Easy. Fill a microwaveable container with 2 cups (500 mL) of water and add a little lemon juice. Microwave on high for three to five minutes.

Refrigerator

"The fridge is often full of old food. Get rid of it."

* Your fridge runs most efficiently when the inside is clean and not over-crowded. Take a quick peek inside the fridge to see what you can send out to the composter.

* Never use harsh cleaners on the inside or outside of any refrigerator surface. Use a soft cloth, warm water, and a mild detergent.

* Use a sturdy chair or small CSA-approved stepladder (and never use a chair on wheels) to reach the top of the refrigerator. Wipe down and replace any objects sitting on top, then wipe the top of the fridge itself. While you're up there, clean any cupboards above the fridge.

* Open the door of the fridge and clean the inner lip and seal of the door and the frame. These surfaces can get mouldy. And if you do see mould, use an all-purpose cleaner. Otherwise, use soap and water to keep it mould-free.

* Wipe the surfaces inside the fridge—the inside walls and shelves. Wipe out the crisper drawers.

* Clean the front and sides and the grate below the door.

* Clean the freezer (when food stocks are running low). Wipe the inside and door panel with warm soapy water.

Body Wise

Try not to slouch while you're cleaning the house. Keep your shoulders square and relaxed, your chest out and stomach in.

Q: There are old spills inside the fridge that won't wipe off easily. Any ideas?

MM: Use a cloth and a paste made from baking soda mixed with warm water (three parts baking soda to one part water). Rinse with water.

Q: What's the best way to keep the fridge smelling clean?

MM: First, make sure to clean out the fridge regularly so that old food gets composted or thrown out when it should. Also, make sure leftover foods are covered properly so that their contents and aromas are contained. For a fresh fragrance inside the fridge, keep an open box of baking soda on the shelf. It will absorb unpleasant fridge smells. And remember to change it every few months.

Stove

"When I'm cooking at the stove, I keep a cloth nearby so that I can wipe up any spills when they happen."

* Clean the stove area. Begin with the range hood and control panel. Clean the top, sides, front, range hood, and fan cover of the stove with a damp cloth and all-purpose cleaner. Clean off fingerprints on knobs and dials. (Take care that you don't turn on the element by accident while you're cleaning this area.) Open the oven door and clean the inside edges of the door.

* If you have a gas stove, soak removable grates, knobs, and handles in a sink full of hot soapy water for five minutes. Flake off food with a soft brush. Rinse thoroughly with clean water. Dry with a clean cloth. Clear the ports of a gas burner stove with a fine wire or a straight pin. Don't use a toothpick, because it can break off and block the port.

* If the stove is electric, remove and soak burner rings and drip pans in a sink full of hot soapy water. This will loosen dirt and make them easier to clean. On the stovetop, clean underneath and watch for rough edges.

* Remember, electric heating elements are self-cleaning and should never be submerged in water.

* Avoid using an abrasive cleaner on the stovetop—it may scratch the surface. Clean smooth-top ceramic and halogen stovetops with the product recommended by the manufacturer, or use hot soapy water and a clean cloth. The surface scratches easily, so be careful if you're wearing rings or bracelets.

* Rinse your cloth often.

* Return to the sink to clean soaking pieces. Dry each piece and put it back where it belongs. And don't wrap drip pans in aluminum foil, since this may cause electrical problems.

* Use glass cleaner to finish with a final eye-catching polish.

Q: Is there an easy way to remove spots from the stove?

MM: There is! For hard-to-remove spots, gently scrape away any excess, and then cover with a generous layer of baking soda. Moisten with water and rub with a damp cloth.

Q: What's the best way to keep a ceramic cooktop clean?

MM: As with all stovetops, wipe up spills immediately with a dry cloth. Be especially careful when you spill food that's high in sugar, such as milk and anything tomato-based—it may etch or discolour the surface. Be sure to clean the surface every day to remove any spills. If you don't clean it daily, the heating and cooling of the surface will make it more difficult to remove spots during regular cleaning. And when you do clean, make sure ceramic cooktops are cool (and never use a wet cloth on a hot surface). Don't set dirty pots and pans on the surface, since they can mark it permanently.

HOW TO CLEAN DIFFERENT COOKTOPS

* *Ceramic.* Your best bet is to check with a kitchen store retailer or department store about specially formulated products for new ceramic and glass stovetops. Otherwise, the rule of thumb is always to use a non-abrasive cleanser on the surface and rub with a synthetic scrubby or sponge. Rinse well with clean water. Buff with a soft cloth for a clean finish.
* *Porcelain enamel.* Wipe the surface around heating elements after each use. Avoid using harsh abrasives or steel wool because they can damage the finish. Use a synthetic scrubby with dish soap and water. It's important to wipe up spills right away because enamel can stain.

Oven

"The oven should be spotless—we definitely shouldn't know what you had for dinner the night before."

* Follow the manufacturer's instructions for cleaning and maintaining your oven, particularly self-cleaning ovens. And be aware that you may nullify your warranty if you use an oven cleaner in a self-cleaning oven. An oven cleaner in a self-cleaning oven will clog the pores in the coating and may damage the surface.

* Commercial oven cleaners are caustic. If you use one for your non-self-cleaning oven, make sure the kitchen is well ventilated.

* Wipe spills inside a cold oven with a warm wet cloth.

* To remove grease, use the degreaser. Spray and let it soak in for a while. Return to clean the grease.

* Broiler pans should be washed after every use. One way to keep them clean is to line them with aluminum foil. Remove the foil after use.

* Remove racks from the oven and scrub them in the sink. For easier cleaning, put oven racks into a plastic garbage bag and spray with oven cleaner. Tie up the bag and let the cleaner work for several hours. Open the bag and wipe down.

* Wipe the walls of the oven with a clean cloth.

Q: Help. I just spilled some of the casserole I'm baking into my hot oven.

MM: Sprinkle salt on it. When the oven is cool, brush off the spill and clean up anything that remains with a damp cloth.

Q: If grease won't come off when I'm cleaning the oven, what do you recommend?

MM: First, use the degreaser and give it time to work. Spray on the spot and let it sit for five or ten minutes. Then try cleaning it off. If the spot still doesn't come off, sprinkle it with baking soda and an equal quantity of vinegar, and scrub gently while the mixture is fizzing.

GREASE NOTES

* Never pour grease down the sink—it can cause blockages. Instead, allow it to cool, then wipe it away with paper towels and scoop it into the composter container or the garbage.

* If grease has caused a problem in the drain, tip 1 cup (250 mL) of salt and 1 cup (250 mL) of baking soda down the drain; follow immediately with boiling water.

EATING AREA

"The eating area is one of those catch-all places in the kitchen. Make sure everyone in the family helps keep it clean."

* Wipe windowsills and baseboards.

* Wash windows and tracks in the eating area.

* Clean any plants and baskets in both the eating area and the kitchen.

* Clean any picture frames, decorative accessories, and switchplates. Always use a stepstool if you need to reach high places. Never step on a counter.

* Spot wash the walls and wipe the door frames, looking for fingerprints.

* Clean the light fixture and/or fan over the table.

* Clean the tabletop. Dust table legs from the top to the floor.

* Clean chairs from the top to bottom—across the top, down the back, the seat, legs, and rungs.

* If there are patio doors, use glass cleaner to clean the glass and be sure to clean the door tracks.

Body Wise

Keep work close to your body. Rather than reaching too far, use a ladder to bring yourself closer to the job. And rather than bending forward from the waist to clean the floor, bend your knees and crouch down.

SINK

"A sparkling clean sink really does set the tone for the whole kitchen."

* Clean around the base of the taps, the taps themselves, the faucet, and the sides, bottom, and drain of the sink. To clean enamel, porcelain, or stainless steel sinks, use a washroom cleaner.

* Scrub the drain carefully. Use a grout brush to clean the drain plug.

* Use a toothbrush to remove any dirt in the edges of the drain or faucet. Rinse thoroughly.

* Give the tap and sink a final polish using glass cleaner and a dry cloth.

Q: Is there a rule of thumb for using a cream or powdered cleanser?

MM: MOLLY MAID recommends using bio-based products for any job you do. But there will be situations where you may have to use something else. For extremely dirty sinks or those with hard or well water, a cream cleanser may be substituted to get the job done. Always check with the manufacturers of your appliances about the cleaners they recommend for their products.

Q: What's the best dish detergent to use?

MM: Many detergents are made with petroleum by-products and contain various additives, including phosphates, that can harm the environment. Look for plant-based environmentally preferable products that are biodegradable and don't contain phosphates, chlorine, or ammonia.

Q: If degreaser doesn't work, how should I remove greasy marks and soap buildup in the sink?

MM: Here's a simple solution to try. For greasy marks and soap buildup, sprinkle baking soda on the sides and bottom of the sink. Then pour a little vinegar over top. While the mixture is fizzing, rub gently with a clean non-scratch scouring pad. Rinse clean with cold water.

Body Wise

The beat goes on: Play your favourite music while you clean. An upbeat, lively tune will keep you happy and moving ... and that will make the work more enjoyable.

KEEP GERMS AT BAY IN THE KITCHEN

Your kitchen sink is one of the dirtiest places in the house. The best cleaning tool in the kitchen is a microfibre dishcloth that you can wash regularly in hot water. MOLLY MAID doesn't recommend sponges for cleaning at all. A sponge is the biggest culprit for germ collection and is not environmentally friendly. Switch to dishcloths.

FLOORS

"As the old saying goes, Your floors should be so clean you can eat off them."

* Move chairs and other furniture to help make sweeping easier.

* Sweep the floor using short strokes and working from the walls to the middle of the room. Make several piles of debris as you go. Pick up debris with a dustpan or the floor attachment of your vacuum.

* Fill a bucket with warm water and 1 capful to ¼ cup (50 mL) of concentrated all-purpose cleaner (check the product directions for recommended ratio).

* Use a cloth to clean the kickboard under the kitchen sink and counters as well as baseboards, corners, and dried-on food stains. Start in the farthest corner and work your way toward the door.

* To wash the floor, start in the farthest corner and work your way toward the door.

* Wash the floor in small sections.

* Use a cloth on the end of the mop handle to reach between appliances.

* Rinse the mop frequently.

* If you have linoleum floors, use a slightly different procedure. Linoleum, which went out of fashion years ago, is making a comeback because it's an environmentally friendly, natural material. If you have a linoleum floor, keep in mind that linoleum is vulnerable to moisture. Use as little water as possible when cleaning it. Use a mop just dampened in water. To remove marks and stains, sprinkle them with a little baking soda and vinegar, then mop.

* Return chairs and other furniture to their original positions.

* Empty the garbage bag and clean the inside and outside of the container with a damp cloth. If there are unpleasant odours in the garbage

can that regular cleaning isn't getting rid of, use baking soda to absorb the odours. Put a handful into the bottom of the garbage can: It will last two to three months.

Q: I've got stubborn scuff marks on my vinyl flooring. How can I remove them?

MM: Wipe them with a damp cloth dipped in baking soda.

MAKING THE KITCHEN SHINE

Once you're finished cleaning the kitchen, make it shine.

* Work your way around the kitchen using glass cleaner and a clean cotton cloth. Remember: Start to the right of the sink and work your way around.
* Buff each object until it shines. Focus on the outside of appliances, chrome, mirrors, and picture-frame glass. Be on the lookout for water spots and streaking—and buff them away.
* Spray glass cleaner into the sink, and dry and buff until the sink looks like new.

QUICK CLEAN

SURPRISE! COMPANY IS COMING AND WILL BE HERE IN TEN MINUTES

There's no time for a major clean, of course, but there is time to tidy and freshen things up. Guests tend to gather in the kitchen, so be sure to give it a quick clean.

* Clean and wipe the counters.
* Put dirty dishes into the dishwasher (or wash and dry them).

* Wipe spills off the stovetop and kitchen table. Wipe the appliances, concentrating on the handles.

* Clean out the sink.

* Sweep the floor and spot wash as necessary.

* Simmer water and cinnamon or other spices on the stove for a warm, lovely aroma.

* Put a flowering plant or bowl of fruit on the counter.

DEEP CLEAN

"When you've got time, there are lots of cleaning jobs that need doing in the kitchen. Once they're done, you'll be glad."

* Search for all old food in the kitchen. Remove any food in jars, bottles, or containers that's past its best-before date. Put compostable foods into your compost bin or discard. Clean and throw packaging into either the recycling box or the garbage. Wipe all shelves in your pantry cupboard with a damp cloth. Next, go through the fridge and freezer. Dispose of old food and leftovers appropriately. Then remove shelves and drawers from the fridge and wash in warm soapy water. Wipe all surfaces with a damp cloth—and don't forget the rubber moulding, since it tends to collect grease and crumbs.

* Pull out the fridge (make sure to ask someone to help you do this). Wipe down the sides and vacuum the condenser coil on the back of the fridge with a soft-brush attachment. Clean the floor underneath.

* Empty drawers and sort through the contents. The cutlery drawer is always well used, and is often filled with crumbs. Remove the cutlery

and vacuum the drawer with a crevice tool. Wipe drawers out. (But don't do all the drawers in one go. It will take forever. Keep tabs on which drawers you do and which ones need to be done. Schedule a few every three months.)

* To clean a self-cleaning oven, refer to the manufacturer's instructions. Clean as much of the grease from the oven as you can. Turn on the cleaning cycle. When it's done, wipe out ashes with a cloth and throw them away. Wipe down the area with a damp cloth. If you don't have a self-cleaning oven, refer to the maintenance and care booklet that came with your oven for its cleaning instructions.

* When the stove is cool, rather than moving it, empty the drawer under the oven (if there is one) and pull it right out. Wash out the inside of the drawer. Vacuum and wipe the now-accessible floor area under the stove. Replace everything.

* If you don't have a self-defrosting freezer, you'll have to thaw the freezer's icy walls before cleaning them. Here's how: Empty the freezer and unplug the refrigerator. Remove the drain connected to a hose on the inside. Leave the door open and put a bowl of warm water inside the freezer. Remove the metal grid at the bottom of the refrigerator and put a rimmed baking dish underneath the drain tube. Shave the ice off the walls using a hard plastic spatula or flipper. (Never jab or hack at ice with anything sharp like an icepick, because you might puncture the wall of the freezer.) Let it melt and drain into the baking dish. If you do have a self-defrosting freezer, turn off the freezer for a little while to warm it up a bit—that way you can wipe its surfaces and the cloth won't stick.

* If windows need cleaning, clean with glass cleaner. Be sure to clean the window track of grime and dirt, too.

* Clean out a few cupboards every time you deep clean the kitchen. Remove everything in the cupboard. Be sure to compost or dispose of any packaged foods that are past their best-before date. Clean the inside of cupboards with soap and water, and then replace contents.

* Follow the manufacturer's instructions to clean espresso machines, and regularly use salty water to rinse any surfaces that come into contact

with coffee. To decalcify the inside, run a mixture of equal parts vinegar and water through the machine, then run plain water through two or three times more.

* To clean your coffee maker, remove and wash the filter basket and carafe with warm soapy water. To descale, pour 2–3 cups (500–750 mL) of water and an equal amount of white vinegar into the water chamber and then turn it on. Turn it off halfway through and let the solution sit inside the chamber for an hour. Turn it back on and finish. Run two cycles of plain water through the machine to rinse out the vinegar. Wipe the outside with a wet cloth. Dry with a dry cloth. And always remember to rinse the inside of your coffee maker well after every use to remove stale traces of yesterday's brew.

* To remove mineral scaling stains from the inside of an electric kettle, fill to cover the element with equal parts of vinegar and water, bring to a boil, allow to cool, then pour out. Boil fresh water and pour it all out before using the kettle again.

* Unplug the electric can opener and use a toothbrush and soap and water to clean the cutting wheel and lid cover. Rinse and dry with a clean cloth. Wipe down the base with a damp cloth.

Body Wise

Never try to move heavy appliances by yourself. Get help.

Kitchen Cleaning Schedule Checklist

EVERYDAY CLEAN

❏ Declutter.

❏ Wipe up spills.

❏ Clear dirty dishes.

❏ Put away food.

❏ Wipe counters and the kitchen table.

❏ Wipe out sink.

❏ Keep garbage and compost containers clean.

❏ Change kitchen dishcloth.

❏ Sweep kitchen floor.

CLEANING DAY

❏ Shake out mats and/or rugs.

❏ Dust ceilings and windowsills.

❏ Clean, dry, and shine all appliance surfaces, range hood, and sink.

❏ Clean stove drip pans, burner grates, and control knobs.

❏ Clean the microwave oven inside and out, including the turntable.

❏ Clean the fridge, wiping shelves and the door rim, where mould often develops.

❏ Wash countertops.

❏ Damp wipe cupboard fronts, table, and chairs.

❏ Compost or discard old food.

❏ Check if windows and other glass surfaces in the kitchen need to be washed.

❏ Clean compost bucket and garbage can.

❏ Clean pets' eating areas.

❏ Collect/empty trash.

❏ Vacuum/sweep floor.

❏ Wash floor.

DEEP CLEAN

❏ Clean under and behind appliances.

❏ Clean closets, cupboards, and drawers.

❏ Clean curtains, other window coverings, and windows.

❏ Compost or discard old food.

❏ Clean the oven, including racks.

❏ Degrease the stove's hood.

❏ Clean refrigerator condenser coils.

❏ Defrost the freezer.

❏ Deep clean small appliances.

❏ Clean out the pantry and fridge.

4
Bedroom

Maybe it's a good time to learn about feng shui?

Feng shui is part of an ancient Chinese philosophy of nature. According to feng shui design principles, all the objects in the bedroom (and the rest of the house) should be in perfect harmony with one another. And one of the most important strategies for achieving harmony is to declutter.

Even if feng shui isn't for you, the bedroom needs to be clutter-free, comfortable, and clean. After all, we spend a third of our lives in bed! Here are ways to achieve a feeling of serenity in the bedroom.

* Surround yourself with objects that make you feel good. Keep family pictures on your bedside table. Keep your grandfather's gold watch by your bedside. Display your daughter's gold-plated baby shoes on your dresser. When you have a calm, peaceful space, a good night's sleep is more likely.

* Decorate the room in warm, comforting colours such as golds, yellows, and reds rather than cool colours such as blues, greens, and white.

* Hang art that makes you feel good—peaceful scenes, for example, that you love or that provide good memories.

* Get rid of the TV. A television doesn't support rest and relaxation, and it discourages communication with your partner. (Maybe there's a guest

bedroom that would be a better place for the television. You can still watch TV in bed if you get the urge!)

* Do your best to keep your closets organized. But keep the closet door closed. The closet is a busy area with footwear and clothing everywhere. It feels cluttered (even if it's not), and clutter affects your ability to relax.

EVERYDAY CLEAN

It's easier and less time-consuming to keep the bedroom clean if you tidy it every day. Everyone in the household plays an important role in keeping his or her bedroom neat, and teaching your children to help out when they're young will be a positive lifelong lesson. And make sure you're a good role model by keeping your own room clean, too. Here are everyday habits that help.

* Hang up and put away clean clothes and footwear.

* Put laundry into the hamper.

* Train pets to stay off beds—or cover beds with throws to protect fabric.

* Keep rooms tidy by going through clutter constantly—are there books, nail files, hair products, and so on that can be put away, recycled, or given away?

* Make the bed every day.

CLEANING DAY

Always clean the room from left to right. Here's a general cleaning checklist, followed by a more thorough guide to cleaning the different areas of the bedroom.

❑ Dust the ceiling and corners with an extendable static duster.

❑ Dust behind doors, and under dressers, desks, and beds.

❑ Dust and clean all surfaces.

❑ Clean surfaces, including windowsills and frames, doors, and switchplates, with a damp cloth.

❑ Clean windows, tracks, and mirrors.

❑ Vacuum or wash the floor.

GETTING STARTED

"Open the window for a few minutes when you start cleaning the bedroom. Fresh air is a wonderful way to freshen up this room."

* Remember, MOLLY MAID cleans a room from the top to the bottom and from the left of the entrance in a room clockwise around the room.

* Remove any small rugs.

* Dust the ceilings and into corners. Carefully dust ceiling light fixtures.

* Hold on to wall hangings, clocks, and other items hanging on the wall with one hand while you dust them with a cloth in the other. That way, you won't accidentally knock things off the wall—and break them.

* Look up so that you don't miss any shelves, knickknacks, and pictures.

* Look down as well. Lower shelves, baseboards, and carpet edges need cleaning too.

* Wipe light switches and switchplates.

* Clean doors and frames. Start at the top of the door frame and clean down the sides. Clean the front, back, and sides of doors.

Q: I have built-in closets in my bedroom with louvered doors. Is there an easy way to clean them?

MM: There are a few good methods to try. Use the brush attachment tool on the vacuum cleaner. Or dampen a clean, soft paintbrush to remove dust from the louvered doors. Or dampen a sock or a cloth and wipe. Kids will love helping with this chore, especially if you put a sock on their hand and call it a dustbug monster!

Cleaning Curtains and Blinds

Window coverings are essential in the bedroom—and keeping them clean is essential, too. Here's how.

Curtains Shake curtains out where they hang, and vacuum to remove the dust. If the curtains are floor length, pay special attention to their hems, where dirt tends to collect.

Windowsills Keeping windowsills clean helps keep curtains clean. Wipe windowsills with warm soapy water. Be on the lookout for mildew around bedroom windows and window tracks, especially when they're closed during the winter. This can trap condensation and lead to the development of mildew.

Roller blinds Vacuum roller blinds with the upholstery attachment. If the blind is waterproof, sponge with a damp cloth or rinse with a little all-purpose cleaner.

Venetian blinds tend to be dust collectors. But no worries. It just means that you have to be extra careful about not missing them during the weekly clean. Here are a few different ways to remove dust. Wear a clean pair of cotton house gloves or an old sock, and run your fingers along each slat to pick up dust as you go. Or turn all the slats to the upward angle and wipe with a damp cloth; then reverse and repeat. The soft brush attachment on the vacuum cleaner also keeps roman and slatted venetian blinds clean. Another way to clean slatted blinds is to use a cloth dipped in water.

Body Wise

Leaning forward without support while you vacuum, sweep, mop, and dust puts a lot of stress on your back. Take a break and stretch out your back by doing a cat stretch. Get down on all fours and, while you contract the muscles in your stomach (the abdominals), slowly round up the back—and hold for five to ten seconds. Feels good, doesn't it?

DRESSERS AND OTHER FURNITURE

"It's amazing how much 'stuff' you can fit on the top of your dresser. Keeping these surfaces sparse and clean makes for a tidier room—and a calmer feeling."

* Damp dust around the room, working with a clean cloth and a bit of water. Wet the cloth and wring dry. If it's too wet, it will leave water marks and streaks. Dust all surfaces, including walls, nightstands, dressers, headboard, footboard, bookshelves, and knickknacks. Dust framed photographs, artwork, and lampshades.

* When dusting any large surface, lift and dust each object, wipe the surface beneath it, and replace. Always bring dust toward you in a side-to-side motion.

* Dust around any books.

* Wipe wooden furniture quickly with a damp cloth.

* Clean mirrors. If mirrors are coated with a thin residue of hairspray and perfume, be generous with the glass cleaner.

* Clean the windowsill and window track. Start at the top, down the sides, and across the sill.

* To dust glass-covered pictures, use a clean cloth sprayed with a small amount of glass cleaner. To dust pictures that aren't covered in glass, use a polishing cloth sprayed with glass cleaner. And for fine art that could get damaged, make sure that you don't use a solvent, since it could harm the finish.

* To clean a lamp, turn the light off. Dust the shade from top to bottom. (Use a clean paintbrush to dust a pleated lampshade.) When the bulb is cool to the touch, reach in and dust the bulb. Wipe the lamp from the top to the base.

BED

"There is nothing like the feeling you get when you climb into a freshly made bed."

* Strip the bed and wash the linens at least once every two weeks.

* Vacuum or wipe all headboards when the bed is changed. Headboards come in a variety of finishes, including wood, veneer, upholstered fabric, and vinyl. Use the appropriate attachment tool.

* Check the wall above pillows for greasy spots that need cleaning (just in case you've got someone who reads in bed a lot and touches the

wall with his or her head). Wipe away with a damp cloth, or spray with all-purpose cleaner and then wipe off.

* Remake the bed using clean linens. (Change the bed once a week if it's really hot weather or if someone is sick.)

* If possible, hang bed linens on the line to dry after you wash them. Fresh, clean sheets that you've dried this way smell divine and are a joy to climb into.

* Air out the duvet and launder if necessary (but there's no need to wash it more than once a year).

* Air out quilts in the sun if possible and launder if necessary.

* Vacuum the valance.

Q: What's the best way to wash a quilt?

MM: Check the manufacturer's instructions first. One thing you don't want to do is wash a feather quilt in hot water or dry clean it. This can make the filling dry and brittle, which may cause it to break up. It might be best to hand-wash or wash on the gentle cycle in cold water. Dry the quilt in the dryer on the air dry or fluff cycle, or hang it up to dry.

Dust Mites Checklist

Dust mites thrive in the bedroom. Here's a checklist to keep dust mites at bay.

❑ Use covers for mattresses, pillows, and box springs.

❑ Ask your doctor or patient association about allergen-impermeable, non-quilted, zippered casings, and where to buy them.

❑ Vacuum regularly and get rid of as many dust collectors in the bedroom (books and bookcases, ornaments, and wall hangings) as possible.

❑ Avoid bulky comforters and chenille bedspreads, which tend to collect dust in their creases. In general, select non-allergenic washable bedding materials.

❏ Wash bed linens weekly in hot water (130°F/54.5°C). For waterbeds, regularly wash the mattress pad on top of the bed.

❏ Replace pillows once a year.

Is Your Pillow Making You Sick?

Body oils build up and bacteria grow in pillowcases, and the bacteria can get passed on to you and cause illness. Make sure to wash your pillowcases frequently. If you have a cold or flu, you should change your pillowcases daily.

Q: Can I wash pillows?

MM: Check the manufacturer's instructions if you're planning to wash a pillow. In most cases you can safely wash pillows either by hand-washing with a mild detergent and cool water or machine-washing using the delicate cycle. If you do the latter, make sure to wash two pillows at a time so that the load is balanced. Tumble dry on the lowest heat setting.

THE NEW WAY TO MAKE A BED

Airing out bedding before you make the bed is now being recommended by health experts. Most people perspire when they sleep, and leaving the bedding exposed helps dry it out. Opening a window to air out the room helps dry sheets too, and it removes humidity. Fresh air prevents condensation problems and discourages dust mites, which thrive in humidity. The new way to make a bed: When you first start cleaning the bedroom, open the window if possible and turn back all the covers on the bed. After twenty minutes, the air in the room will have been exchanged and the mattress and linens will be fresher and drier. Teach everyone in the family this new rule.

FLOORS

"Whether floors are carpeted or bare, it's
important to keep them clean and to get rid of
the dust balls."

* Remove throw rugs and vacuum or sweep bare floors, starting in the corner farthest from the door.

* Fill a bucket with hot water and add all-purpose cleaner. Soak a wet cloth in the bucket and wring it out. Wipe the baseboards and into the corners.

* Mop or wash the floor and be sure to rinse the mop or cloth often.

* If there are streaks, dry them with a clean cloth.

* Replace throw rugs.

Q: My dog sleeps on the rug beside the bed. Is there a special way to clean the rug? It smells like the dog.

MM: It would be great if you could install a dog bed where your four-legged friend likes to lay its head at night. That way you could wash the bed periodically to keep things clean. Otherwise, invest in a good rug shampoo and follow instructions. In between shampoos, use baking soda to help absorb some of the doggy smell. Sprinkle the area with baking soda (you can even buy scented baking soda products for your rugs). Let it sit for five to ten minutes, then vacuum.

HOW TO PREPARE A GUEST ROOM

* Open the window to air out the room.
* Strip the bed.
* Dust and vacuum.
* Make up the bed with fresh bed linen.
* Leave out a spare pillow and blanket.
* Leave a bath towel and hand towel folded on the bed.
* Clear some space for clothing—in the closet and cupboard if possible.
* Make sure there's a working bedside lamp and a wastebasket.
* Leave out a photo album, crossword puzzle book, or magazine—just in case your guest can't sleep.

Yikes! Bedbugs

There has been a lot of news about the reappearance of bedbugs in metropolitan areas. Just keep in mind that the presence of bedbugs doesn't mean you're not clean enough. Bedbugs often enter a home transported in clothing, luggage, or other household items, and they're not looking for garbage; they're looking for blood.

What do they look like? Bedbugs have a brown, wingless oval body and a short, broad head. They are broad and flat and about 6–10 millimetres long. After feeding, they swell slightly in size and darken to a blood-red colour. Nymphs are shaped like the adults, but are yellow-white in colour.

Bedbugs typically feed at night when people are asleep. Itchy welts on skin, blood spots on sheets, and/or black or brown spots on mattresses, bed frames, or walls are all signs.

To prevent an infestation, always be cautious about taking in second-hand furniture, bedding, mattresses, or beds. Inspect these items carefully—the seams, tufts, and crevices. Remember that bedbugs prefer wood and fabric to metal or plastic. As well, wrap mattresses in zippered bed casings, available from allergy supply companies or mattress stores, or wrap and seal in plastic film.

If you do detect bedbugs, every room in your house will need a good cleaning, especially the bedrooms. Here are treatment strategies.

* Wash mattress pads and sheets in hot water and dry them on the high setting. You may have to remove the cloth underside of the box spring to determine if there are bedbugs inside.

* Scrub surfaces with a stiff brush to dislodge eggs, and use a powerful vacuum to remove bedbugs from cracks and crevices. Dismantle and clean bed frames.

* Remove drawers from desks and dressers and turn furniture over, if possible, to inspect and clean all hiding spots.

* Vacuum with a brush attachment. Dispose of the bag immediately afterwards.

* Steam clean carpeting.

* Vacuum upholstered chairs and sofas, too. Launder cushions, slipcovers, skirts, and so on.

* Remove clutter. Bedbugs hide in minuscule areas, and any belongings left lying around provide a perfect opportunity for them to hide and continue to breed.

* You may want to call in a pest control professional.

Getting Your Kids to Clean Their Rooms

Recruit your children to help with basic cleaning routines, especially in their own bedrooms. Regularly following a routine will develop good organizational habits in your children, and will reduce your own stress caused by having to remind children time and again to tidy their rooms. Here are some suggestions.

* Make up a cleaning kit that contains all the essential supplies and materials needed to clean each room. Store it in a brightly coloured plastic bucket. Make sure cleaning products are kid friendly and age appropriate.

* Help them tidy the room to show them how it's done.

* Provide teenagers who have accumulated a lot of stuff with plastic bins or baskets for their possessions. But suggest they keep the bins in the closet. For younger children, keep a toy chest at the end of the bed for toys and games. Plastic bins or baskets can also be used to help eliminate clutter—store these in a closet.

* Rearrange the furniture with the child. Involving children in design decisions allows them to take ownership—and possibly responsibility—for helping to keep the room clean. And rearranging the furniture is also a great time to do a thorough clean.

* Use your children's ideas when decorating their rooms. If they like the decor, the room will be more comfortable and fun for them … and they'll be more likely to keep it clean.

* Be consistent with the cleaning routine. For example, remind children every night before bed to tidy up their rooms so that they're neat for the morning.

* Make sure to tell your children how proud you are of them, and that they're doing a great job.

Body Wise

Protect your body from too much strain by looking for a simpler solution. For example, instead of straining your arms and shoulders to dust away cobwebs on the ceiling, use a ladder or invest in an extendable duster.

Is It Time to Give Your Children's Toys a Bath?

Toys can become contaminated with all kinds of nasty things. Here's a guide to keeping toys clean.

* Wash plastic toys in warm soapy water from time to time. They can also go into the dishwasher, on the top rack, on a normal wash cycle.

* Check washing instructions, but soft toys generally can be washed in the washing machine on a delicate cycle. Put them into a pillowcase and knot the top to protect the toy.

* Freshen up a soft toy by sprinkling it with baking soda and shaking gently. Leave it for an hour or so, then vacuum the powder away or shake and pat the toy gently.

* Wash soft toys that can't be machine-washed with a slightly damp cloth.

QUICK CLEAN

SURPRISE! COMPANY IS COMING AND WILL BE HERE IN TEN MINUTES

If visitors ask for a tour of the house, you'll want the bedrooms to be clean and tidy. Here's how to tidy up a bedroom in almost no time.

* Put away clean clothes, put dirty clothes into the hamper, and hide the clutter—in a box in the closet.

* Put obvious trash in the garbage.

* Straighten out the bedspread and fluff up pillows. Remove anything from the top of the bed that shouldn't be there.

* Either open the curtains (and let the sun in) or draw the curtains and turn on a bedside light.

* Dust nightstands and clean the surface of clutter.
* Pick up any large pieces of dirt and/or dust bunnies visible on the floor.

DEEP CLEAN

"Cleaning your bedroom is a liberating experience! When all the clutter is gone, there's a calm, clean feeling in the room—and that's what you want in a bedroom."

* Clean windows and tracks. Spray glass cleaner on the glass. Take a cloth and wipe across the entire surface.
* Turn the mattress at least twice a year.
* Launder the mattress cover.
* Vacuum the mattress.
* Replace pillow covers.
* Wash pillows.
* Wash duvets (in preference to dry cleaning).
* Wash the valance.
* Launder or dry clean curtains. Don't wait too long to launder your curtains. When fabric is really dirty, it's tougher to get it clean.
* Sort through your wardrobe and drawers.

Is It Time to Clean Out Your Drawers?

In a perfect world, your drawers would be clean, tidy, and orderly all the time. Here are tips on keeping drawers in good order.

* When you buy something new, be sure to get rid of something old.

* Clear out contents from time to time by going through each drawer and recycling or discarding items you no longer use.

* Clean out one drawer every month in order to stay on top of clutter. The goal is to fit things easily into your drawers. It's easier to be tidy that way.

* Return your clothing and other items to their place at the end of every day if possible.

* Use drawer-lining paper, or even wallpaper, to help keep drawers and clothes clean. And scented paper will keep clothes smelling great.

* One way to determine which clothes in your closet to keep is to hang them all on hooks facing into the closet. As you wear them, rehang your clothes on hangers facing out. After a few months, look closely at the clothes you haven't worn. Maybe it's time to get rid of them. Donate them to a local charity, which helps the environment because you're recycling.

Bedroom Cleaning Schedule Checklist

EVERYDAY CLEAN

❏ Declutter.

❏ Make bed (everyone is responsible for his or her own).

❏ Put clothes away.

❏ Put dirty laundry in hamper.

CLEANING DAY

❏ Shake out scatter rugs.

❏ Change bed linens.

❏ Collect/empty trash.

❏ Dust the ceiling and corners.

❏ Dust behind doors, and under dressers, desks, and beds.

❏ Dust and clean all surfaces.

❏ Clean surfaces, including windowsills and frames, doors, and switch-plates, with a damp cloth.

❏ Clean windows, tracks, and mirrors.

❏ Vacuum and/or wash the floor.

DEEP CLEAN

❏ Clean windows and tracks.

❏ Turn the mattress at least twice a year.

❏ Launder the mattress cover.

❏ Clean the bedskirt.

❏ Vacuum the mattress.

❏ Replace pillow covers.

❏ Wash duvets.

❏ Wash the valance.

❏ Launder or dry clean curtains.

❏ Sort through your wardrobe and drawers.

❏ Clean blankets, duvets, and pillows.

❏ Polish frames of pictures and mirrors.

❏ Shampoo carpet.

5
Living Room / Family Room
Dining Room

In most homes, the rooms where we spend a lot of our downtime are the rooms that need constant cleaning. The living room is often where family and friends visit (sitting around and drinking coffee together, and so on), are entertained (by a sound system or television), entertain themselves (with puzzles, games, or a book), or just relax. And when children and pets are part of the household, furniture and furnishings take an even heavier pounding. For this reason, it's a good idea to buy furniture that's practical in design and solidly built. Perhaps furniture should be covered so that pet hair doesn't get over everything. The colour of furnishings is an important consideration, too. Most moms will tell you that it's a smart idea to go with a colour that doesn't accentuate tiny fingerprints and paw prints. And did you know that patterned upholstery conceals dirt better than solid fabric? As well, wall surfaces and coverings should be washable.

Child- and pet-proofing a home also means keeping valuable display pieces such as expensive bowls and vases out of reach. You'll need safe storage for these kinds of items until children are older and pets are trained.

On the other hand, if kids are older or you don't have children (and there's little risk of a mishap with a thrown ball, for example), you may be more apt to have a traditional living room where precious objects are on display. Colour isn't as big a concern either. Choosing white or a pale colour palette won't be an issue (although the room will need more conscientious cleaning).

When the living room is combined with the dining room, there's often more work to keep them both clean. People naturally move between the two rooms in a way they wouldn't when the dining room is set apart and used only for dining.

It all adds up to the importance of regular cleaning, a realistic schedule, and, some days, a sense of humour.

EVERYDAY CLEAN

It's easier and less time-consuming to clean the living room, family room, and dining room when you keep them tidy on a regular basis. That way, you're maintaining cleanliness rather than starting from scratch every time. Here are everyday cleaning habits that help.

* Keep a handheld vacuum nearby to vacuum crumbs.

* Avoid leaving newspapers on your couches and chairs. The print can transfer onto the fabric.

* Always put away items that shouldn't be there. For example, fold and stack any scattered newspapers and magazines, pick up toys, and take dirty dishes to the kitchen.

* Plump cushions on the couch to prevent creases. Creases accelerate wear and can trap dirt. And, of course, plumped cushions make a seating area more inviting.

* Arrange furniture so that it's away from windows and radiators, since exposure to direct light and heat can cause fabrics to fade. Otherwise, make sure to close blinds when the sun shines in.

* Arrange furniture 6 inches (15 cm) from walls instead of flush against them so that there'll be fewer smudges from bumping to look after later. You'll also have easier access to corners that need cleaning.

* Wipe pets with a cloth when they come in from outside to reduce the amount of dirt that ends up on rugs and upholstery.

* Keep pets off upholstered surfaces, or cover furniture with throws to protect the fabric.

* Open and close blinds, curtains, and other window coverings often. This helps to displace dust so that it falls to the floor.

* Always remove dishes and food from the table after the meal.

* Leave placemats on the table and ready for the next meal if that makes mealtime easier, but be sure they're clean and crumb-free.

* Keep a tray or basket on the dining room table that holds napkins, salt and pepper shakers, and any other spices or condiments you like to leave on the table.

* Keep rooms tidy by going through them constantly and looking for knickknacks, empty flower vases, DVDs, and so on that you can get rid of or put away.

CLEANING DAY

Here's a general cleaning checklist, followed by a more thorough guide to cleaning the different areas of these rooms. The rule of thumb is to clean each room from top to bottom and left to right.

❏ Dust the ceiling and corners with an extendable static duster.

❏ Dust behind doors, and under tables and other furniture.

❏ Dust and clean all surfaces.

❏ With a damp cloth, clean surfaces, including windowsills and frames, doors, and switchplates.

❏ Clean windows and mirrors.

❏ Sweep or vacuum.

GETTING STARTED

"Cleaning is a great physical workout ... talk about getting your ya-yas out!"

As in every room, the MOLLY MAID method of cleaning is from top to bottom and left to right. It's the quickest and most efficient way to clean, and we recommend the system for all cleaning tasks. You'll always know what you've done and, therefore, make more efficient use of your time and do a more thorough clean.

* Remove scatter rugs and shake outside. Hang over a line. Gently beat out dust and leave to air.

* Dust the ceilings and into corners. Carefully dust ceiling light fixtures, including ceiling fans.

* Damp dust around the room, working with a clean cloth and a bit of water. Wet the cloth and wring dry. If it's too wet, it will leave water marks and streaks. Use a dry cloth to polish if necessary. (Be careful where you set the bucket—you don't want to leave marks. Place the bucket on a clean dry cloth.)

* Dust all surfaces, from walls and baseboards to tables and the television. Dust framed artwork, photographs, and knickknacks.

* Clean doors and frames. Start at the top of the door frame and clean down the sides. Clean the front, back, and sides of doors.

* Vacuum and clean windowsills. Start at the top and clean down the sides and across the sill.

* Use a soft, lint-free cloth and glass cleaner to clean all glass or mirrored surfaces. Wash the inside of all windows and their tracks with a damp cloth and window cleaner. Rinse and dry thoroughly.

* Wash or clean all window coverings (blinds and draperies) following the manufacturer's instructions.

Q: I've got screens in my windows. What's the best way to clean them?

MM: Try using one of the vacuum attachments—it often does the job. Otherwise, it's a bigger job to remove the screen from the window to clean it. How to do it: Place screen on a flat surface and scrub with a mixture of 1 capful to ¼ cup (50 mL) of concentrated all-purpose cleaner and a bucket of warm water (check the product directions for recommended ratio). Spray the cleaner off with a hose, shake off excess water, and put the screen back in place to dry fully.

FURNITURE AND FURNISHINGS

"It's amazing what I've found between the pillows of the couch—there are always crumbs, but I've also discovered books, a Barbie doll, and my favourite bracelet!"

* Clean wall units and other large furniture from top to bottom. First, lift and dust each object; then dust the back of the shelf, then underneath and behind. Start with the top of the unit and dust down to the bottom. You may need a stepladder—use it safely.

* Dust around any books.

* Use a damp cloth to remove dust from wooden furniture.

* Treat tabletops like shelves. Remove everything from the table. Dust and wipe the table. Always bring dust toward you in a side-to-side motion. Dust and shine each object you've removed from the table and replace. Dust under the tabletop, then dust the sides and legs, from top to bottom.

* Use a clean paintbrush or vacuum cleaner attachment to remove dust from carvings and mouldings.

* To clean a lamp, turn the light off. Dust the shade from top to bottom. (Use a paintbrush to dust a pleated lampshade.) When the bulb is cool to the touch, reach in and dust the bulb. Wipe the lamp from the top to the base.

* To dust a framed picture, use a polishing cloth. Start by wiping the top of the frame, working down the side and across the bottom. Always spray glass cleaner on your cloth and never directly on the glass to prevent seepage under the glass that could damage the picture.

* Dust and clean plant leaves by wiping gently with a damp cloth.

* Remove all cushions from couches and chairs and vacuum from top to bottom, including sofa base, sides, and armrests. Vacuum underneath the couch or chair. Vacuum the cushions, then replace them. If the cushions don't come off, make sure to vacuum between and behind them if possible.

Q: Should we wax furniture?

MM: Overpolishing with wax can create a buildup. So, no, don't wax furniture every time. While wax isn't going to hurt your furniture, it takes more effort to apply and shine polish than it does to remove dust. Remove the dust with a damp cloth.

Q: My mother always oiled her teak furniture. Should I do that too?

Polished and unfinished teak is a soft wood and needs to be oiled. Here's how: Apply raw linseed or teak oil with a soft, fluff-free cloth or paintbrush. Let it soak in. After a few minutes, redistribute the excess oil to the drier areas and wipe away any residue with the cloth.

Q: Are there special cleaning instructions for leather furniture?

MM: Leather is actually more durable and easier to clean than fabric. Spills can be wiped away quickly. Always refer to the manufacturer's care advice before attempting to remove stains. To remove dirt and dust, wipe leather upholstery with a barely damp soft cloth.

How to Clean Upholstered Furniture

To remove dust from upholstered furniture, use the furniture attachments that come with your vacuum cleaner. If the cushions come off your sofa and chairs, remove them and vacuum those areas first. (Make sure to pick up any large items you find in furniture first, as well as coins!) After you've vacuumed underneath the cushions, do the backs and arms. Make vertical passes starting at the top. Then vacuum the outside areas of the furniture, moving from top to bottom. Now vacuum the cushions on all sides. Fluff them up and put them back on the furniture (rotate them if possible to reduce wear).

For stains, special stain removal products are available at hardware and home supply stores. Always follow the manufacturer's instructions. It's important to test this type of product in a hidden spot on furniture—just to be sure the product won't fade or otherwise damage the material.

If you notice that your furniture looks as if it needs a more thorough cleaning, perhaps it's time to contact a professional cleaning service.

CLEANING THE FIREPLACE

It's important to have your wood-burning fireplace or stove professionally cleaned and serviced at least once a year. Soot and creosote build up in a fireplace and chimney and are potential fire hazards. And between professional cleanings, there's a lot you can do yourself. To clean, wear protective gear such as goggles and gloves, and cover the surrounding surfaces to protect them from soot. Sweep or wet/dry-vacuum the walls and ceilings of the fireplace as well as the hearth, and remove as much soot as possible. Use a stiff-bristled (not wire) brush dipped in clean water to scrub surfaces. For heavy buildup, use water with a little all-purpose cleaner added. But always rinse thoroughly in case the residue is inflammable. Clean fireplace doors with window cleaner—you may need to carefully scrape off creosote with a razor's edge. Always use extreme caution when using this type of tool. Clean doors help improve heat transfer and prevent deterioration.

Body Wise

While you're dusting, window washing, and doing other housecleaning chores, make a point of switching hands. We often use our dominant side to do chores ... but this can lead to overuse injuries.

HOME ELECTRONICS

"I wipe off dust every time I use the stereo. It's a start to keeping things clean."

* Always check the owner's manual for instructions regarding the care and cleaning of your electronic equipment, including the stereo, speakers, television, and DVD player.

* Gently remove dust from the front of stereo speakers with a barely damp cloth or with the vacuum hose and flat attachment.

* Dust the outsides of electronics with a soft dust-mop cloth lightly moistened with dishwashing liquid and water. Never use any abrasives or solvents on metal.

* Use a glass cleaner sprayed on a cloth to clean the top, sides, and control panels and to wipe the shelf in front of stereo equipment. Remember that dust shows up quickly on shiny dark surfaces.

* Never spray cleaning products directly onto home electronics.

* Spray the vents of equipment with a can of compressed air to remove dust.

* Wipe the dock of an iPod or other rechargeable electronic device with a damp soft lint-free cloth.

* Clean remote controls with a damp cloth—wiping the entire surface, including the front, back, sides, and buttons. (It's important to clean surfaces that are touched a lot because they're transfer sites for germs.)

* Dust the surface of the stereo with a damp cloth.

* Use a dry electrostatic cloth or sponge to dust screens of plasma, LCD, and standard TV sets in long horizontal strokes starting at the top of the screen.

* To clean the TV, use a cloth to dust the top and sides, then a damp cloth to clean the TV cabinet and frame only. Use the soft-brush attachment of the vacuum cleaner to remove dust from the ventilation grilles at the back of the TV.

* Treat CDs and DVDs gently to avoid damaging the shiny reflective surface. Hold a disk by inserting your finger or thumb inside the centre hole, or handle it by the edges. To remove dust, wipe the disk gently with a soft cloth. Always wipe in a back-and-forth motion from the centre to the outer edge, *not* following the disk's concentric circles.

Q: My two-year-old got hold of a favourite DVD with her sticky fingers ...

MM: Mix some baby shampoo with lukewarm water and use a lint-free cloth to gently wipe the disk's surface. Make sure the disk is completely dry before returning it to its case.

FLOORS

"Whether floors are carpeted or bare, it's important to keep them clean and to get rid of the dirt and dust."

* Vacuum or sweep bare floors starting in the corner farthest from the door.

* Hardwood floors are easily scratched, so use protection pads on the bottoms of legs and other heavy furniture.

* If you have bare floors, lift and move furniture rather than sliding it to avoid scratching the floor. If you have carpeted floor, slide furniture (don't lift), vacuum, then move it back.

* Use a crevice tool to edge carpet and corners for dust and pet hair. Wherever possible, use attachments to vacuum underneath heavy furniture.

* Vacuum frequently, and make sure to include carpet cleaning in your annual deep-clean schedule. Change your vacuum bag habitually, too. Carpets are a favourite breeding ground for allergens such as germs, skin cells, pet hair, fungi, and dust mites. And keep in mind that the machine doesn't function well when the vacuum bag is full.

* Fill the bucket with hot water and add 1 capful to ¼ cup (50 mL) of concentrated all-purpose cleaner (check the product directions for recommended ratio). Soak a wet cloth in the bucket and wring it out. Be sure to keep a dry cloth under the water bucket in order to protect any surfaces on which you place the bucket.

* Wipe the baseboards and into the corners.

* Mop or wash the floor, and make sure to rinse the mop or cloth often.

* If there are streaks, dry them with a clean cloth.

* When the floor has dried, replace the vacuumed mats.

Body Wise

As you vacuum, try to avoid bending over. Maintain an upright posture, and instead of pulling the vacuum, guide it along in front of you as you go. And, of course, to avoid tripping, hold the cord in one hand.

Q: I've got dark hardwood floors throughout my home. What's the best way to clean them?

MM: Check with the flooring manufacturer, if possible, to find out what cleaning product is recommended. Otherwise, mop with a slightly damp mop or cloth, using plain water. Never wet-mop a wood floor or leave water on it. And don't use furniture polish!

Q: I just spilled grease on my carpet. Now what?

MM: Pour a generous amount of baking soda over the grease and brush lightly over the soiled area. Leave it on overnight and vacuum the next day.

Q: I've come across a wad of old chewing gum on the carpet. Is there an easy way to get it off?

MM: There sure is! Use ice in a bag and freeze the chewing gum. When it becomes brittle, shatter it and vacuum up the broken pieces.

Dust Mites

There's no getting around it—everyone's house has dust mites. But some have more dust mites than others. It depends on whether you're feeding them well or not—with dust.

Dust mites are microscopic bugs that love dust because it contains small particles of plant and animal material that they eat. While dust mites aren't disease carriers, their droppings can trigger a range of allergy and asthma symptoms in different people.

Where are dust mites found? They tend to live in carpets, mattresses, and pillows. They thrive in high humidity and in areas where human dander (dead skin flakes) is located (the bedroom and other rooms).

It's impossible to get rid of dust mites completely, but you can do a lot to control them. The key is to clean your house regularly. Here are ways to keep them at bay.

* Mites love humidity! Keep the humidity below fifty percent throughout the house with a dehumidifier or central or window air conditioning.

* Minimize dust collectors in your house (dust collects on books and bookcases, ornaments, and wall hangings).

* Use enclosed bookcases and curio cabinets instead of open shelves.

* Use washable throw rugs—and wash them regularly in hot water or have them dry cleaned.

* Use a damp cloth when dusting to minimize airborne dust.

* Minimize the use of upholstered furniture: vinyl or leather is preferable.

* Buy washable toys for your children.

* To help remove airborne allergen particles, use an air cleaner with a HEPA (high-efficiency particulate air) filter.

* Use a central vacuum if possible, or an efficient vacuum with a HEPA filter. And don't forget to change the vacuum cleaner bag on a regular basis.

* Clean the furnace and all air ducts regularly.

* Use an air conditioner in the summer or screened window ventilators to keep out dust and pollens. Vacuum the dustproof casings regularly.

* If you're allergic to dust mites, wear a dust mask when cleaning.

QUICK CLEAN

SURPRISE! SOMEONE JUST CALLED TO SAY YOU'VE BEEN ELECTED TO HOLD AN EMERGENCY MEETING IN YOUR LIVING ROOM IN TEN MINUTES

Here's how to do a quick clean.

* Declutter. Store—or hide—anything that doesn't belong in the room in a container, a box, or even a closet. (You can put items in their place later.)

* Make the couch look inviting and comfortable. Brush off cushions. Plump the pillows.

* Dust tabletops, including the dining room table and coffee table.

* Clear the coffee table. A flowering plant or a bowl of fresh fruit would be nice …

* Dust all other surfaces, including electronics, books, blinds, and pictures.

* Clean fingerprints from all surfaces, including doors and switchplates.

* Sweep or vacuum—just the floor. Don't worry about moving furniture.

DEEP CLEAN

* If you have a chandelier or other elaborate light fixture in the living room or dining room, it's important to clean it thoroughly from time to time. Check with a light fixture company to see if they sell special cleaner for chandeliers. Otherwise, here's how to clean it: Turn off at the switch and give the light bulbs time to cool down. Place a large plastic bag or sheet on the table or floor and cover that with newspaper or a towel. Without dismantling the chandelier, lift a small container filled with a mixture of hot water and glass cleaner, immerse each pendant for a few seconds, and allow to drip dry. Alternatively, put hot water and a little glass cleaner into a spray bottle. Spray the pendants and allow them to drip dry. Of course, you should never immerse bulbs or electrically wired components of chandeliers in water—dry-dust these parts instead.

* Ceiling fans tend to get coated with a thin layer of dust. For this reason, and especially at the end of each season, they need a good deep clean, too. Turn off the ceiling fan and lay plastic and an old sheet underneath it on the floor or table. Stand on a ladder safely, and use a handheld duster to dust as well as possible around the base and fan arms. Angle the head, if you can, to dust the tops of the blades. Wipe them with a cloth sprayed with all-purpose cleaner. Be sure to unscrew the light fixture, if the fan has one, and wash it in the sink with warm water and dishwashing liquid. Rinse and dry before reattaching.

* Most fabric lampshades can be dry cleaned. Clean washable lampshades in the bathtub if they're too big for the laundry sink. Be careful, though: The fabric may be washable, but the glue that holds the shade together may not be.

* If you have bookcases in your living room, remove all the books and dust the shelves thoroughly.

* To clean fluorescent and track lighting, dust the hardware and bulbs with an extendable duster. Unscrew the metal ceiling mounts and wipe with a cloth wet with water and dishwashing liquid. Reattach.

* Clean curtains. Dry clean if necessary; otherwise, launder according to the manufacturer's instructions.

* Clean blinds. Remove the entire blind and soak in soapy water in the bathtub lined with a towel (to protect the tub from scratches). Use a scrub brush or sponge to clean. Use a handheld showerhead to rinse. Stand to dry in the shower. When almost dry, wipe with a dry cloth so that there are no water marks. In the summer, clean blinds outside on the lawn with a hose. Let the sun dry them.

* If furniture has coverings, follow the manufacturer's instructions to wash them.

* Rotate seat and back cushions to ensure even wear and uniform fading.

* Consider steam-cleaning upholstery and rugs yourself.

* Clean out the drawers and cupboards of the dining room buffet and other cabinets or cupboards you use for storing good china, cutlery, serving dishes, and so on. This type of storage tends to get messy, dusty, and disorganized over time, so take a good look at what you have and keep only the items that you really want and need.

Body Wise

Clean lights safely. Always unplug lamps before cleaning, and never plug in any appliance with wet hands—this puts you at risk of an electrical shock. And if cords are frayed, don't plug them in again, either. If cleaning wall-mounted lights, turn off the electricity at the fuse box.

Living Room / Dining Room Family Room Cleaning Schedule Checklist

EVERYDAY CLEAN

❑ Declutter.

❑ Wipe up spills.

❑ Clean up after pets.

❑ Clear off table.

❑ Sweep floor.

CLEANING DAY

❑ Dust ceilings, walls, and windowsills.

❑ Dust behind doors, under tables, and other furniture.

❑ Dust and clean all surfaces, including windowsills and frames, doors, and switchplates.

❑ Dry-dust stereo, TV, and other electronics.

❑ Clean dining room table.

❑ Vacuum carpets, stairs, and upholstery.

❑ Clean lamps.

❑ Clean windows and mirrors.

❑ Sweep or vacuum.

❑ Wash floor.

DEEP CLEAN

❑ Clean under furniture.

❑ Shampoo carpets and upholstery.

❑ Clean out cabinets and drawers.

❑ Clean curtains and other window coverings.

❑ Deep clean lighting fixtures.

❑ Dust and clean books.

❑ Polish wooden furniture.

❑ Polish frames of mirrors and pictures.

❑ Clean (and reverse) ceiling fan blades.

6
Home Office

It seems everyone has a home office these days, whether it's a designated area in the family room or kitchen or a spare bedroom that doubles as the computer room. Some homes even have "home offices" set up in the area under the stairs, the upstairs landing, a loft, or a non-working area of the kitchen. At the same time, an increasing number of people are officially working from home these days. With the cost of transportation (both in stress and in dollars) and the sophistication of telecommunications, it makes sense. So if you're one of those people, it's important to make sure that your home office is light, airy, nicely decorated—and clean. As Laurence J. Peter, an American educator and author, said, "If a cluttered desk is the sign of a cluttered mind, what is the significance of a clean desk?"

EVERYDAY CLEAN

It's easier and less time-consuming to keep your office clean if you keep up with the clutter and garbage—and that can be a challenge.

* Keep the desk as tidy as possible. Desktop organizers such as mini-sorters, letter trays, and storage trays can help.

* Keep a blue box or bag next to the garbage can so that you can sort recyclables from garbage on the spot.

* Make sure you've got a filing cabinet and enough bookshelves so that you can put away office clutter at the end of every workday.

* When you've turned off the computer at the end of your workday, run a damp cloth over the keyboard, screen, and back of the monitor so that it's clean and ready for the next day.

* Do a walkabout of the room to check for items that don't belong there—and toss them all into a basket. As you head to the kitchen, return them to their rightful spots.

* Don't ever use your desk as a dinner table. Spills can happen, and they can cause permanent damage.

CLEANING DAY

Always clean the office from the left to right. Here's a general cleaning checklist, followed by a more thorough guide to cleaning the different areas of the office.

❑ Dust the ceiling and corners.

❑ Dust behind doors, under the desk, and in cupboards and closets.

❑ Gently dust equipment in the office, including the computer, screen, keyboard, mouse, fax machine, printer and cables, and wiring and power bars under the desk.

❑ Dust and clean pictures and the bulletin board if you have one.

❑ Wipe down all surfaces. With a damp cloth, clean the desk, windowsills and frames, doors, and switchplates.

❑ Clean windows.

❑ Vacuum or wash the floor.

GETTING STARTED

"When you work at home, you need your work area to be clean. Try to tidy at the end of every day—just as at the office."

* In the office, you'll need the all-purpose cleaner, window cleaner (if there's a window), and disinfectant (for the telephone).

* Dust the ceilings and into corners. But be careful when you dust the ceiling over the computer—you don't want dust to fall into the back of the computer or onto the keyboard.

* Hold an item with one hand while you dust with the other. This helps prevent breakage when you're dusting pictures, clocks, and other items hanging on the wall.

* Look up so that you don't miss any shelves, knickknacks, and pictures.

* Look down as well. Lower shelves, baseboards, and carpet edges need cleaning too.

* Wipe light switches and switchplates.

* Clean doors and frames. Start at the top of the door frame and clean down the sides. Clean the front, back, and sides of doors.

Body Wise

To avoid the spread of germs, clean the mouthpieces and keypads of your phones regularly. Wipe with a slightly damp cloth.

THE ROOM

"When the office is a mess, I have trouble concentrating on the work I have to do. It's better to start every day in a clean office."

* Dust light fixtures with an extendable duster.

* Vacuum curtains or other window coverings with a brush attachment.

* Wash the windows and tracks with glass cleaner. Wipe the sill and frame with a damp cloth.

* Dust filing cabinets, tables, and other furnishings with a damp cloth.

* Vacuum the office chair with a brush attachment. Wipe down legs, arms, and wheels of the chair with a cloth. Clean dirt off the wheels. If the base and legs of the chair are plastic, use a little lemon oil on a cloth and buff to bring up the shine.

* Dust the bindings of books.

* Wipe the outside of storage containers with a damp cloth.

* To dust lamps, turn the light off and let the bulb cool to the touch. Dust the shade from top to bottom. Reach into the light and clean the bulb, the inside of the shade, and the lamp base.

Q: My home office is in the basement. How do I get rid of mould and mildew?

MM: Home offices are often located in the basement, especially in smaller urban homes. And subterranean usually means moisture—and possibly mould. Mould and mildew are caused by moisture that gets trapped in places with little or no ventilation. Basements are prime targets, especially if there are leaks in the foundation. Small areas of mould and mildew can be cleaned with a detergent solution. Some experts recommend wearing a mask, safety goggles, and rubber gloves when doing this type of work. Seek professional help if there's a lot of mould, or if mould comes back after cleaning. To avoid the problem, keep a dehumidifier running, especially during the summer—if you don't have air conditioning or even if you do. If you've been away for a week and the dehumidifier hasn't been running, leave an open box of baking soda where the smell is strongest.

THE DESK

"It's amazing how much stuff you can fit on the top of your desk."

* Gather loose objects on the desk, and either pile them in one corner or put them somewhere else.

* Dust the desk carefully from top to bottom. Dust the entire empty surface of the desk, and always bring dust toward you in a side-to-side motion. If the desktop is glass, spritz a cloth with glass cleaner and wipe. If the desktop is metal, use all-purpose cleaner. If the desktop is wood, use a damp cloth and wipe in the direction of the grain to prevent streaking.

* Dust the frame and legs with a damp cloth from top to bottom.

* Clean the phone. (Considering how often people touch the phone, it can be a breeding ground for germs.) With a slightly damp cloth, wipe the telephone keypad, handset, and cords. Use a cotton swab dipped in disinfectant to clean the keypad and buttons. Spray a little disinfectant onto a cloth and clean the handset.

* To clean the fax machine, spray compressed air at about forty-five degrees into the rolling mechanism inside the fax to blow out dust. Compressed-air cleaner products are available at most computer stores.

Q: What's the best way to remove coffee stains from the fabric of my office chair?

MM: Douse black coffee stains with soda water and blot, don't scrub—that will usually remove a fresh stain.

Organize Your Desk for Work

Clear some space Give yourself a large enough desk where there's room for your basic office tools, the phone, and the computer. This is where you compose sales pitches, open mail, and review files and books, so there has to be enough room for everything. If there isn't enough room, consider getting a second desktop for either your computer or a workspace. You won't get much done if you feel squeezed for space. In most home offices, the computer monitor, keyboard, and mouse form the central grouping of the desk, with other essentials positioned around this group. When setting up or reorganizing your desk, focus on the essentials. (But don't forget the personal touches, such as a few framed pictures of family members.)

Order your tools Group together tools such as pens and pencils, a stapler, and a tape dispenser. Check out an office-products store for a wide range of organizers. These include memo clips, letter trays, three-tier desk shelves, and mini-sorters. Keep your various office tools in some type of box or organizer on your desk or in a drawer—rather than loose on the top. That's how clutter builds. Periodically check pens, pencils, and markers and toss the ones that have run dry.

Control the flow Develop a system for looking at incoming work and disposing or dispensing of work you've finished—you can buy an in-and-out box system. These can be wire, steel, plastic, or wooden trays that are part of coordinated desk sets.

Sort your mail A mail organizer is a good idea, too. Your home office will be receiving all kinds of mail: bills, catalogues, and so on.

Utilize storage Make use of the space under your desk with drawers and other storage. Keeping things out of view is a great idea. But don't let drawers become clutter buckets. Keep drawers as organized as possible. Consider the function of each one when you store office items. The top drawer should hold tools you use every day, such as pens, the calculator, the stapler, and so on.

Tuck it away A keyboard tray attached to the underside of the desk is a great space saver. Does it work with your setup? What's most important is that you make sure the keyboard is ergonomically at the right height for you. If it's not, be sure to adjust the height of the chair. When you're not using the computer, the keyboard ideally slips underneath and out of sight.

Body Wise

Some health experts favour household activities over regular exercise because they're productive and health promoting. So instead of going for a jog or walk, grab the duster or floor mop and get some exercise cleaning the house. This type of activity helps you stay in shape, too.

COMPUTER

"Your computer is one of your most important business tools. Treat it with respect—and a clean cloth."

* The cleaner you keep your work space, the cleaner your equipment will be.

* The best way to clean any computer component or device is to follow the manufacturer's instructions in your user manual. Remember to turn your computer off before cleaning.

* Never spray cleaning fluids directly on computer components. Always spray the cleaner on a cloth, then wipe.

* Remove dust and crumbs from computer keyboards with a soft brush or vacuum cleaner attachment. Another way to do this is to turn the keyboard upside down and gently shake it. Do this over a garbage can or towel that you can shake out, because most of the crumbs and dust will fall out. You can also use compressed air to spray between the keys to remove loose hair and dirt.

* Use a cotton swab dipped in warm soapy water and patted dry to clean keys.

* Rub the top and bottom of your mouse with a paper towel dipped in rubbing alcohol. Take off the bottom and remove the ball. Blow dust from the casing with compressed air, then wipe the ball and interior with a cotton swab dipped in alcohol. Let the ball dry before replacing it and closing the mouse.

* Use compressed air to remove dust from all external surfaces.

* Wipe the monitor screen gently with a damp/dry cloth to remove dust and fingerprints. Never touch the back of the monitor.

* Regularly vacuum the back and front of the computer's hard drive to remove dust from openings. Accumulated dust can cause the fan to work overtime, which may cause the computer to overheat.

Q: Help! I just accidentally dumped a glass of water into my keyboard.

MM: You've probably ruined it, but here's what you can try: Disconnect the keyboard immediately, or if you have a wireless connection, quickly turn off the computer and remove the batteries from the keyboard. Flip the keyboard over to drain. Flip back and blot the top with a paper towel. Blow compressed air between the keys and leave it to air dry overnight. (And cross your fingers.)

CLEANING WITH COMPRESSED AIR

Compressed air is pressurized air in a can with a very long nozzle. Simply aim the air between computer keys, for example, and blow away all the dust and debris that has gathered there. A vacuum cleaner uses air as well to clean, but it sucks dirt rather than blowing it out. If you use a vacuum for the keyboard, make sure there aren't any loose, easy "pop-off" keys that could possibly be sucked up by the vacuum.

Q: Can I really wash my keyboard in the dishwasher, as I've heard?

MM: There is one company that makes a waterproof keyboard, so make sure the label states that the keyboard is dishwasher safe. Otherwise, never put your computer keyboard in the dishwasher to get it clean. Once the keyboard gets submerged in water, the wiring can lose functionality.

Q: Is there a special way to clean a computer monitor?

MM: Carefully, of course! Monitors that are made of glass and don't have any special coatings can be cleaned using water or a basic glass cleaner. Never spray any liquid directly on the monitor—the liquid could run down into seams and into the electronics. Spray on a soft, lint-free cloth just enough cleaner to moisten, and gently wipe the viewable surface. You can use a computer vacuum or compressed air to remove dust from the monitor housing, paying special attention to the vents. Cleaners may damage the plastic casing of your monitor, so use a cloth slightly moistened with water.

Surface Advice

Computer glass screen Use a soft clean cloth and gently wipe the screen. Spray cleaner on the cloth, not on the screen. Caution: Never spray or squirt any type of liquid on any computer component.

Soft screens (LCD) Use only a dry soft clean cloth and wipe gently. Do not use any solvents.

Projection television Check the manufacturer's suggestions and use a dry soft clean cloth. Caution: Do not use cleaners or water.

Windows (this is great how-to advice for cleaning windows in any room, of course) Spray glass cleaner sparingly on the surface. Use a clean dry lint-free cloth (preferably microfibre). Fold the cloth in four (so that there are actually eight surfaces for cleaning). Change the cloth when it becomes wet and soiled. Don't overwipe the glass. Quickly wipe and allow to dry. If needed, polish and dry the glass surface with a clean dry cloth.

FLOORS

"Whether floors are carpeted or bare, it's important to keep them clean and to get rid of the dust balls."

* Pull lightweight furniture out from the wall so that you can clean underneath.

* Vacuum or sweep bare floors starting in the corner farthest from the door.

* Fill the bucket with hot water and add 1 capful to ¼ cup (50 mL) of concentrated all-purpose cleaner (check the product directions for recommended ratio). Always put a dry cloth under the water bucket in order to protect the surface it's on.

* Soak a wet cloth in the bucket and wring out. Wipe the baseboards and into the corners.

* Mop or wash the floor and be sure to rinse the mop or cloth often.

* If there are streaks, dry them with a clean cloth.

* Wash the chair mat.

Q: Would a chair mat for the office chair make cleaning easier?

MM: It would. The purpose of a chair mat is to protect the carpet or floor from wear and tear caused by the chair constantly moving in and out from the desk. There are chair mats made specifically for hardwood as well as low- and medium-pile carpets. As for cleaning, floor mats are usually vinyl and cleaning is a cinch—use a damp cloth and all-purpose cleaner for the best results.

Making Your Home Office Work for You

If you're officially working from home, a dedicated office helps condition your mind that this is where you work. If you're able to renovate, consider converting the attic, basement, or garage into a home office. Here are tips and strategies for the best—and cleanest—work space you can get.

Give yourself a nice workspace You'll be spending a good deal of time at your desk, so rather than relying on second-hand and makeshift furniture, buy proper furniture and equipment that will provide the correct ergonomic positioning for you. And, if it's a nice workspace, you'll feel some pride and want to keep it tidy.

Let the light in It's always important to work where you have enough light. If there aren't enough windows, be sure to provide both task and ambient lighting. Ambient lighting from overhead lights and floor lamps—especially in a basement—offers overall light, while task lighting (the desk lamp) allows you to see your work.

Make sure you can breathe Your office needs to be properly ventilated, which will help keep you alert and working well. The first choice of course is fresh air from an open window. Alternatively, run a fan to keep the air moving.

You need peace and quiet The office area should provide a quiet spot to work. Therefore, it should be situated as far as possible away from potential distractions such as the kitchen, the front door, family traffic, and other noise.

Integrate the space If you have to create a home office area in an existing room, a few tricks can help you integrate it into that space. If your kitchen is clean and contemporary, use a stainless steel table and chair and keep supplies in containers that are not unlike the kitchen's, such as cookie jars. Keep binders and files on a rollout cart placed under the desk. If the office is tucked into a corner of the living room, incorporate files into bookshelves but make sure they're contained in attractive boxes. Also, choose a desk in a material similar to the furniture (such as mahogany or painted white) so that it blends seamlessly. Push it flush against the bookshelf so that it doesn't stick out. And use the desk chair—an attractive leather one, for example—as an extra living room seat.

Is everything accessible? The design and layout of your home office should facilitate efficiency. Arrange office supplies for convenience—and tidiness. Daily-use items should be kept close at hand, either stowed under the desk or in small see-through drawer units on top. Store office supplies such as paper, tape, scissors in cabinets, if there's space, or in baskets on a nearby bookshelf. Wall-mounted shelving offers a lot of storage without having clutter on the floor or desk, and it's easy to install. Just make sure that whatever you put up is matching and in good shape, or it will distract. A wall-mounted phone near your desk will make desk space available. Keep machinery free of obstructions—a stack of paper in front of your printer is going to block incoming documents. And the printer should always be within easy access—on the desktop or under the desk if it's on a small printer stand.

Is everything organized? Using a "zone" system helps keep the office tidy. Have a zone in your office for all paperwork. Keep all your paper there, including sheets for the copier and printer, as well as the mail, magazines, bills, envelopes, stamps, and your chequebook.

Apply a finishing touch Treat the home office as part of your home decorating scheme. Look for attractive wall colours and furniture materials, play up any natural light, and select task lighting that's in keeping with the overall decor of the house. And tie in the material on your desk chair to that of any other furniture in the room, even if you have to custom-make slipcovers for the office chair. Art is an important part of your office, especially if you work in the basement where the scenery isn't too wonderful. But remember that visual clutter, too, can be distracting. If you've carved space out of an existing area of your home, make sure that you can either move yourself out of sight or position yourself in your desk chair so that you don't see the entire room. Alternatively, you could set up an artistic screen or room divider to create your own cubicle.

Body Wise

Since housework often involves a lot of twisting and turning, be sure to wear loose, comfortable clothing when you're cleaning. And wear something old and worn so that you won't have to worry about getting it dirty!

QUICK CLEAN

YOU JUST PUT THE PHONE DOWN ... AND HAVE AN UNEXPECTED MEETING WITH A CLIENT IN TEN MINUTES IN YOUR HOME OFFICE

Don't panic. Clients don't expect your home office to be perfect, but they do expect a certain level of professionalism. First and foremost, it's got to be clean. Here's how to tidy up your home office in almost no time.

* Put obvious trash in the garbage.

* Put used coffee mugs and other food dishes and packaging in the kitchen.

* Wipe the computer and the casing.

* Dust the tops of filing cabinets and bookshelves.

* Stash stray office supplies such as pencils and pens in decorative stationery boxes or filing containers on your desk.

* Pick up any large pieces of dirt and/or dust bunnies visible on the floor.

DEEP CLEAN

* Dust and wash the mouldings.

* Dust and wash door frames and handles.

* Have someone help you move heavy pieces of furniture such as the desk and filing cabinets, and vacuum or mop underneath them.

* Clean out closets.

* Wash switchplates and doorknobs.

* Remove books from shelves and dust them and the shelf before replacing.

* If old books are starting to smell musty, here's a great way to freshen them up. Put the book into a shoebox with an open box of baking soda. Close the lid and let it sit for two days. The baking soda will absorb the mildew smell.

* Spray the printer, keyboard, and other equipment with compressed air to clear away dirt.

Home Office Cleaning Schedule Checklist

EVERYDAY CLEAN

❏ Declutter.

❏ Wipe up spills.

❏ Sort garbage.

❏ Leave desk tidy.

CLEANING DAY

❏ Dust ceilings and walls.

❏ Shake out and dust curtains and other window coverings.

❏ Dust and clean all surfaces.

❏ Collect/empty trash.

❏ Wipe off telephones.

❏ Clean and buff surfaces (mirrors, windows).

❏ Clean lamps.

❏ Clean office equipment.

- ❏ Wipe office chair.

- ❏ Vacuum carpets, rugs, and stairs.

- ❏ Vacuum or sweep bare floors.

- ❏ Wash floor.

DEEP CLEAN

- ❏ Dust and wash all surfaces.

- ❏ Clean under furniture.

- ❏ Shampoo carpets and upholstery.

- ❏ Clean out filing cabinets and other office storage.

- ❏ Clean curtains and other window coverings.

- ❏ Deep clean lighting fixtures.

- ❏ Dust and clean books.

7
Laundry Room

The laundry room is often one of those catch-all areas in the house that fills up with all kinds of household items—sports equipment, empty boxes, not to mention laundry and containers of laundry soap! While it's great to have a place to put stuff that you don't know what else to do with, no one wants to work in a room where there's that much chaos. Furthermore, it can be dangerous when you have to watch every step you take!

Now's a good time to stand back and think about how to better organize and manage the laundry room. Perhaps a stacked washer and dryer would fit the space better? Can you create a storage closet for the odds and ends that fill the room now? A few bins or other storage cupboards and cabinets may be all you need to tidy this room once and for all.

Here's a quick guide to help you keep the laundry room functioning—and tidy.

EVERYDAY CLEAN

It really is easier and less time-consuming to keep the laundry room organized day by day.

* Clean the lint trap every time you use the dryer.

* Keep a small garbage container in the laundry room (rather than letting lint and other garbage pile up on the dryer).

* Wipe off the tops of the washer and dryer with a damp cloth.

* Leave the lid of the washer open for twenty minutes or so after using it so that moisture will evaporate, leaving no opportunity for mould or mildew to develop.

* Always wipe spills rather than letting drips run down and create a mess on the liquid soap jug and the surface it sits on. Be sure to keep a cloth handy for these types of spills.

* Keep cleaning products organized in a cupboard or on a shelf nearby— and, of course, out of reach of children.

* Fold up dry laundry and put it away (rather than letting it sit in or on top of the dryer or elsewhere).

Body Wise

When you're cleaning, it's important to wear supportive shoes in order to protect your feet. Leave the slippers in the closet, and never clean in your stocking feet!

CLEANING DAY

- ❏ Wash and dry dirty clothes that are in the laundry room and put them away.

- ❏ Put away clutter that shouldn't be in the laundry room—return items to their storage area or create a storage area.

- ❏ Dust walls and cabinets. Use a long-handled mop if necessary or a dry cloth.

- ❏ Wipe the outsides of the washer and dryer with all-purpose cleaner and a cloth.

- ❏ Open the lid of the washer and use a microfibre cloth sprayed with all-purpose cleaner to clean the softener and soap dispensers and any other surfaces that need cleaning.

- ❏ Clean the tops of any counters or work tables with a damp cloth.

- ❏ Wipe out the laundry sink with a damp cloth.

- ❏ Sweep or vacuum the floor.

- ❏ Shake out scatter rugs or mats.

- ❏ Wash the floor.

DEEP CLEAN

"Airing out dirty laundry—and a dirty laundry room—is good for the soul."

* Remove and shake out scatter rugs. Vacuum and/or wash these mats or rugs if they need cleaning.

* Dust, starting with the ceiling.

* Dust mouldings and baseboards.

* Go through all your laundry products and dispose of any outdated products. (Check with your municipality about how to dispose of them safely.) Then organize what remains. Set up shelves, cabinets, and bins so that you can safely store the products and items you need nearby.

* Remove the lining bag from the hamper if there is one, and wash it in the washing machine.

* Wipe the inside of the hamper with a damp cloth or vacuum it with a brush attachment.

* Wipe out plastic laundry baskets with a damp cloth.

* Rinse out the detergent and softener container in the washer with water so that it won't get clogged.

* Clean the lint trap insert in the dryer. Remove lint with a damp cloth or wet your hands and run fingers over the mesh screen to scoop up lint. Vacuum the mesh screen with a brush attachment on a low setting, or wash it in a sink with water and a little dishwashing soap. Dry it before replacing it.

* Pull out the washer and dryer and vacuum the backs as well as the floor underneath. Be sure to get help moving these heavy appliances. Don't stretch the dryer hose, though; disconnect it if necessary.

* Vacuum the heating and air-conditioning vents.

Q: Is there an easy way to wash out the washer?

MM: Keep it clean and smelling fresh by filling it with water and adding 2 cups (500 mL) of vinegar. Let the washer sit for an hour that way, then restart it and allow it to go through the wash and rinse cycle. (You could throw in the scatter rugs before you restart the washer so that it doesn't feel as though you're wasting the water.)

Q: And the dryer?

MM: Wipe the interior walls with a damp cloth. That's all you should need to do. If there's any linty residue around the trap opening, scrub that with a toothbrush.

Q: My iron has spray-starch buildup on its base. Is there an easy way to clean that off?

MM: Wipe it down with a paste of baking soda and water (three parts baking soda to one part water) applied to a cloth. Use cotton swabs to work the paste around the holes. That should do the trick!

Body Wise

Always make sure that the floors you've washed are dry before you walk across them—since wet floors are slippery, they represent an accident waiting to happen.

Organizing Your Laundry Room

Keeping your laundry room organized will make wash day feel a little less chaotic. Here's what you need to put into place.

Central hamper Make sure there's a hamper in a convenient spot in the house—probably near the bedrooms. Choose one that has a liner bag that comes out easily or one that doubles as a laundry basket (meaning it's light enough to carry around). Another good idea is to set up a spot in the house for items needing dry cleaning—if your family uses the dry cleaner a lot.

Sorting bins Sort laundry in the laundry room by setting up three bins—labelled darks, lights, and delicates. Visit a store that specializes in storage bins and containers and choose the right-sized containers for your space. You'll find tubs on wheels, lightweight hampers, and large baskets that fit into shelving units. Another idea is to use laundry bags—label three and hang them close to the washer and dryer.

Shelving and other storage Set up shelving for detergent and other products you use for the laundry. If you have small children, it's a good idea to put these products into a locked cabinet or one that's out of reach of little hands. Keep a container there for care-label instructions as well as stain-removal information. The whole point is to locate all the information and products you need for laundry in one convenient spot. You'll never go looking for anything again! Shelving and other storage in the laundry area is also a good place to keep clothes pegs for hanging laundry outside as well as hand-washables soap, special stain-removal products, and mesh bags for delicate laundry. Keep in mind that appliances are now available with built-in lower drawers. This type of drawer is an ideal location for cleaning and other laundry products (not ones you want to keep from kids, however). The drawer means the appliance is higher, which is easier on your back since you won't have to bend to do the laundry. It might also be a good idea to install a cupboard or closet of some kind that can hold all the household cleaning supplies and tools, including the mop, broom, dustpan, and so on. This is a good place to store your ironing board and iron as well. A fold-down ironing board can be stored out of sight.

Drying area Before throwing clothes into the dryer (and *not everything* goes into the dryer), consider whether they're better off drying on an indoor drying rack or retractable clothesline that can work in the basement or laundry room. It's important to have a place inside to hang clothes to dry in such a way that people aren't walking through them. For clothes that need to dry flat, you'll need a surface of some kind. Consider buying a special drying rack or installing a good-sized shelf. At the same time, hanging clothes outside is the best-case scenario—you're not using electricity, and laundry smells fabulous when it has dried outside.

Folding area The designated folding area should be kept clean—and clear. An old table does the trick. Some people use the appliances themselves as a folding surface, although this can be tricky because you're bound to lose socks and other small items down the side. (Some people also like to carry their dry laundry to the family room and fold laundry while they watch television—if that works for you, just be sure to put the folded laundry away when you're done.)

Garbage can Make sure to have a garbage can near the dryer—or else fluff from the filter will end up on top of the washer and dryer.

SAVE ENERGY
Read the how-to instruction booklet for your dryer so that you're using the different energy-saving programs properly.

Laundry Room
Cleaning Schedule Checklist

EVERYDAY CLEAN

❏ Declutter.

❏ Wipe up all spills immediately.

❏ Sort and wash laundry.

❏ Fold and put away clothes.

❏ Clean out dryer lint trap.

CLEANING DAY

❏ Shake out scatter rugs/mats.

❏ Wipe appliances down.

❏ Clean insides of appliances.

❏ Clean folding table and other surfaces.

❏ Collect/empty trash.

❏ Sweep or vacuum floor.

❏ Wash floor.

DEEP CLEAN

- ❏ Dust ceiling down to floor.

- ❏ Wipe out hampers.

- ❏ Clean laundry bags.

- ❏ Clean behind washer and dryer.

- ❏ Repaint floor if it's cement.

- ❏ Clean products shelf or drawer.

- ❏ Clean out storage.

While you're in the basement:

- ❏ Check batteries in smoke detectors (annual).

- ❏ Change furnace filter (as per manufacturer's recommendations).

- ❏ Schedule professional maintenance of heating/cooling units (annual).

8
Pets in Your Home

You've probably heard that people who have pets generally live longer, have lower blood pressure, and are less stressed. But pet owners generally have more housecleaning chores, too. And cleanliness is critical, not just because of unpleasant pet odours but also for good health. The good news is that there are lots of ways to keep a pet's home clean as clean can be!

Keeping a Pet-Friendly Home Clean

The task of keeping your house clean when you have pets can be divided into daily maintenance to keep hair and dust levels down and occasional cleanups after an accident. Since most dogs and cats shed their hair, proper grooming is the first and most effective step in keeping down dust and hair in the house. Here are other effective ways to keep a pet-friendly home clean.

* Choose a designated sleeping area for your pets—a bed they can call their own. Hair will be more contained to just one area.

* Place carpet underlay beneath the pet's dishes to keep them from sliding around and spilling.

* Try to shake out your pet's bedding on a daily basis, clean around its bed twice a week, and launder its bed once a week.

* To keep cats from using your furniture as a scratching post, spray the arms and legs of the sofa or chairs with perfume—they hate the smell. Check with a pet store for other deterring options.

* Keep a scratching post for cats—and try to teach cats to use it (it will save your furniture and keep cats happy because they love scratching).

* If pets lie on the furniture, use washable covers if possible to protect against animal hair and soiling.

* Microfibre mops are effective at picking up hair and dustballs from the floor.

* To pick up pet hair from furniture, try Scotch tape or masking tape rolled backward around your fingers. A pair of rubber gloves, a chamois, or a damp cloth will also do the trick.

* Special vacuum cleaners have features that remove animal hair. Also, since hair seems to gather around the edges of furniture, use an edging tool or the straight hose to get those spots first, then vacuum the rest of the furniture.

* Hair rakes, available from the pet store, will remove a lot of hair before vacuuming to keep things gentle on carpets.

* Gauze or cheesecloth placed over air vents keeps hair from circulating through the ductwork, making it easier to keep dust down.

Body Wise

Have you ever found yourself hauling the vacuum, your cleaning products, and some items from the garage ... all at the same time? Instead, be kind to your back, and make a few separate trips. That way you can also protect yourself from tripping and injuring yourself.

* Line the pet bed with a towel to catch hair and dirt—this is easier to pick up and wash than the whole bed.

* Keep an old towel at the back or front door to wipe pets down on rainy, muddy days. A small scatter rug at the back door will catch what dirty paws leave behind.

* Because cats like to walk on counters—where food is also prepared—scrupulous cleaning is necessary!

* Make sure your pet is up to date on preventive medications for fleas and ticks—to avoid an infestation. Follow instructions for administering medication.

* Clean and disinfect pet cages regularly. Do this in the bathroom, laundry room, or outside.

* Take five minutes at the beginning or end of the day to pick up after the animals—vacuum their hair off the sofa, clean up drips of water near the water dish, and sweep the pet food from the kitchen floor.

* For keeping up with the mud and dirt tracked in by your pet in the spring and fall, invest in several long towels—buy used, if need be—and leave them by the back door. Use two as a runner to soak up the immediate dirt, especially on wet days, another to wipe the dog down, and the other two to have a backup for when the floor "runners" need laundering.

How to Eliminate Pet Hair in the House

The more frequently you brush pets, the more hair ends up on a brush and not on your floors or furniture. Here are other suggestions.

* Brush the pet outdoors.

* Cover pillows and mattresses with impermeable anti-dust-mite covers.

* Use a HEPA air filter in the bedroom and family room, and on the vacuum (or use a central vacuum system).

* Wipe all surfaces with a damp cloth (to pick up hair).

* Consider getting rid of carpets. Non-carpeted floors prevent the accumulation of pet hair.

Accidents Will Happen

All pets, especially puppies, have the occasional accident. When an accident does happen, deal with it immediately—because if it dries, the odour will remain. Even if you don't smell it, other animals will, and again, this is an open invitation for them to mark their "territory" right on top of the accident spot.

For urine, use a specially designed product available from any pet supply store. It contains enzymes that break down organic wastes and neutralize odours. Don't use ammonia-based cleaner—it smells like urine to your pet and will actually encourage the pet to be a repeat offender.

Blot up the accident right away with a cloth, a paper towel, or even a baby diaper (this works really well), and clean the spot with a cloth soaked in soda water to help eliminate the odour. Then rinse the affected area. If the stain reappears a few days later, sprinkle baking soda over the spot and vacuum when dry.

If your pet has vomited, clean it up immediately. Use a scraper to lift up as much as you can, then get the rest with paper towels, a damp cloth, and gentle bath or baby soap to dab out the mark.

Body Wise

Dogs are man's best friend ... but they can shed a lot of hair and create dust in the house. One way to reduce the pet hair is to brush your dog regularly. (The nice thing about this is that most dogs love getting brushed ... so it's win-win!)

Q: How do I get rid of skunk smell?

MM: Ask a pet store about specially designed shampoos.

Q: I've just discovered that my dog has fleas.

MM: There are two things you must do: gain control of the infestation in the house, and help your pet get rid of its fleas.

For the house, Health Canada recommends vacuuming on a daily basis to remove eggs, larvae, and adults. Be sure to include the following areas: carpets, cushioned furniture, cracks and crevices on floors and along baseboards, and the basement. Steam-cleaning carpets may also help, since the hot steam and soap can kill fleas in all stages of the life cycle. As well, it's important to pay attention to where pets sleep. Wash all pet bedding and family bedding that pets lie on in hot soapy water every two to three weeks. Adult fleas may lay eggs on the host, which then fall off in those areas where pets rest. Lift blankets by all four corners to avoid scattering the eggs and larvae. If an infestation is severe, discard old pet bedding and replace it with fresh, clean material.

To help the pet get rid of fleas, contact your vet about products that will help.

ALLERGIES AND PETS

Pets provide companionship, security, and a sense of comfort to many families. While dander and saliva are the source of cat and dog allergens, urine is the source of allergens from rabbits, hamsters, and guinea pigs—so make sure to give the task of cleaning the animal's cage to a non-allergic family member. The most obvious way to combat symptoms of animal allergy is to avoid or minimize contact with the pet. Vacuuming helps remove some dander. Using a HEPA vacuum filter or double bags may help. If you have a pet-friendly house, consider getting rid of rugs and living with a hardwood floor, tile, or linoleum.

Pets in Your Home Cleaning Schedule Checklist

EVERYDAY CLEAN

❑ Pick up after pets in the house (toys, leash, etc.).

❑ Clean up after pets (in the yard).

❑ Clean off pets (when they come into the house).

❑ Clean pets' eating and drinking bowls regularly.

❑ Brush pets.

❑ Clean out litter box.

CLEANING DAY

❑ Deep clean eating area.

❑ Remove hair from furniture.

❑ Shake out pet's bedding.

DEEP CLEAN

❏ Bathe pets.

❏ Clean out doghouse.

❏ Wash pets' bedding.

9
Outside the Home

Malcolm Gladwell, the author of the bestselling book *Blink*, says that a person makes a decision in the two seconds it takes to blink an eye. But that decision isn't as offhand as it sounds, explains Gladwell. It's actually formed quickly, he says, out of a reservoir of accumulated knowledge in our brains.

Now what does this have to do with cleaning?

Everything. When someone approaches your home, what they see in the first split second is the impression that starts to shape their opinion of you. Perhaps garbage or recycling bins are lying across the driveway or leaves are blowing all over the lawn. Is the garage door open—showing disorganization and mess? Perhaps the porch is untidy, with cobwebs in the corners. Or windows and windowsills are coated with dirt and dust. Like it or not, all these things contribute to people's first impression of you and your home. Even though family and true friends still love you, keeping the outside of your home clean and well maintained is important. It also teaches your immediate family a thing or two about the importance of clean. We recommend a swept walkway, a clean mailbox, and a blemish-free front door.

EVERYDAY CLEAN

It's easier and less time-consuming to keep the outside of your home clean if you keep up with the clutter and garbage—and that's a challenge.

* After the garbage truck has been by, put the cans back where they belong rather than leaving them tossed where the garbage collector left them.

* Teach your children to put away skateboards, boots, bikes, and so on where they belong—and not leave them outside in the front yard or on the porch.

* Pick up stray papers and garbage blown in by the wind as you come into the house.

* Have a garbage container in the car and get your children to use it.

* When you clean out your garage or other rooms, plan ahead so that the garbage can be taken right away rather than cluttering up your driveway for days. Check the trash pickup schedule in your community.

* Install a bench or storage container on the front veranda and use it to store and conceal outdoor play items or gardening tools used in the front yard.

Body Wise

When you're cleaning, it's important to take breaks. Pour yourself a glass of water or a cup of tea and take a five-minute break.

CLEANING DAY

❑ Sweep the front veranda.

❑ Wash outdoor windows near the front door.

❑ Sweep the walkway from the driveway and around to the backyard.

❑ Put away garbage and recycling bins.

❑ Be sure the kids put their bicycles in the garage or around the back.

❑ Throw away or recycle old lawn equipment that doesn't work anymore.

GETTING STARTED

"The outside of your home is a little different to clean than the inside. But it's just as gratifying when it's done!"

* Assemble tools and make sure they're all in working order. You may need an extendable ladder, scrub brushes with handle attachments, cleaning cloths, an outdoor wet/dry vacuum with an extension cord or outdoor plug, old towels or rags, access to water, a bucket, and your regular cleaning products. And be sure to wear old clothing, because you'll be getting wet and dirty.

THE FRONT VERANDA

"Sitting on the front veranda after dinner has become a tradition in my family. And it's got to be clean."

* Remove and shake out the door mat.

* Dust the front of the house, removing any cobwebs and other dust.

* Vacuum wicker and cane furniture to remove dust within the weave. If dirt is stubborn, loosen with a stiff brush—a toothbrush also works. Wash furniture with warm soapy water, rinse with a soft cloth and clean water, and let it dry.

* Wash windows and their tracks around the front door.

* Sweep the front veranda, starting in the far corner and working toward the steps.

* Sweep down each step.

* If it makes sense, wash the floor of the porch and the steps.

Body Wise

Washing your hands regularly is the best way to avoid the spread of germs.

Q: How do I get old decals off windows?

MM: Spray with warm water or glass cleaner, then scrape away with a scraper or old credit card.

WALKWAYS

"Keeping your walkway clean is almost as good as having a new walk."

* Sweep stone paths that run the perimeter of your home with a stiff broom.

* Clean walkways with a power washer or outdoor hose. Keep the hose down, moving the water toward the garden. Start at the top of the path and move toward the street level.

THE PATIO AND GARDEN

"The patio is an important part of entertaining and enjoying our home. In fact, it's an extension of our home in the warmer weather."

* At the beginning of the season, clean decks, gazebos, play structures, and pergolas of dirt, debris, and any layers of surface mould that gets very slippery when wet. Start by sweeping off surface dirt, especially between planks and on facing boards, to keep up airflow and reduce standing water. Then clean with a long-handled scrub brush and soapy water. Follow with a clean water rinse.

* Have a cover made out of plywood to keep raccoons and neighbourhood cats from doing their business in the sandbox.

OUTDOOR FURNITURE

"Enjoying the outdoors from a pretty perch requires more than having the right equipment and nice landscaping—you need clean seats, too."

* Clean plastic or vinyl furniture with soap and water.

* If furniture is aluminum, clean it with a mix of water and mild dish-washing detergent. Follow with a spray from the garden hose. Avoid abrasive cleaners or steel brushes, which scratch aluminum.

* Clean wrought-iron furniture with water and mild dish detergent. It can rust over the winter, so use vinyl covers for protection or bring it inside.

* Clean teak furniture with a soft scrub brush and soapy water. Teak weathers naturally to a soft grey, but if you want to bring back the original colour, talk to an expert about using a water-based teak protector.

* Chrome furniture needs to be cleaned with a damp cloth and dried thoroughly to keep it free of rust. If there are marks, rubbing lightly with baking soda will remove them.

Body Wise

Since cleaning can involve some pretty rigorous activity, it's important to warm up all your muscles beforehand. Try walking or lightly marching on the spot for five minutes—or walking up and down the stairs a few times. (And carry various items that need to go up and down the stairs while you're at it.)

Q: How do I remove scuff marks on my outdoor plastic furniture?

MM: Sprinkle baking soda on scuff marks and rub it in with a damp cloth. (But if the furniture has a high-gloss finish, don't use baking soda because the finish will get scratched. Try a pencil eraser instead.) If scuff marks still don't come off, buy a plastic lawn furniture paint (ask at your local hardware or home supply store)—and paint over them.

QUICK CLEAN

SURPRISE! YOUR BEST FRIEND IS STOPPING BY WITH AN ICED COFFEE TO HAVE A CHAT ON THE FRONT VERANDA

Although best friends usually come around to see you and not the state of your home, it's a sign of respect and welcome to do a little cleanup ahead of time.

* Quickly sweep the front porch, steps, and front walk with a stiff broom.

* If you have a mat under your porch furniture, give it a quick shake over the porch rail.

* Wash off the porch table with all-purpose cleaner and shine it up.

* Make sure seats are clean—and if they're not, wipe them down. (Put cushions on the seats if you have them.)

* Put obvious trash in the garbage.

* Run a duster over the windowsills.

* Pick flowers from your garden and place them in a pretty vase on the porch table.

DEEP CLEAN

"Depending on the season, there's always something to clean up outdoors."

* Vacuum window screens and under the sills.

* Clean tracks and wash windows with glass cleaner.

* Dust stained-glass windows with a clean soft brush, then wipe with a damp cloth. (Don't use any harsh cleaner such as ammonia or vinegar.)

* Wash outside doors.

* Sweep and clean off the porch.

* Wash the outside of basement windows and tracks (and clean wells of debris and dead leaves).

* Attach a power nozzle to the garden hose and wash out garbage containers, recycling bins, and large plastic plant pots. Spray down the driveway, walkway, retaining walls, fences, cement porches, and patios.

* If you have a dog and a doghouse, clean it out regularly—and more frequently during rainy and humid times. Wear rubber gloves to pick up feces around the structure and to remove the bedding. Remove all pet toys, and soak them in a container of warm soapy water. Take off the structure's roof, if possible, and sweep the inside clear of branches, leaves, and dirt. Then scrub with a brush and hot soapy water, making sure to get into the corners and edges. Rinse with the garden hose.

Outside the Home Cleaning Schedule Checklist

EVERYDAY CLEAN

❏ Pick up garbage.

❏ Put away sports and other equipment.

❏ Put garbage and recycling bins away.

❏ Put away garden tools.

CLEANING DAY

❏ Dust outside veranda.

❏ Sweep veranda and walkways.

❏ Wipe down garden furniture.

❏ Wash windows that need washing.

❏ Clean mailbox.

DEEP CLEAN

☐ Clean windows (check weather stripping and seals).

☐ Clean the exterior, including doors.

☐ Wash the veranda.

☐ Clean grills, patio furniture, and other seasonal equipment (summer and fall).

☐ Inspect and clean out garages, basements, lofts, and sheds.

10
Cleaning Different Surfaces

Here's an A to Z resource guide to cleaning counters, floors, and walls. Of course, it's always prudent to check with a manufacturer, if possible, for the recommended cleaning procedure. Keep in mind that in some cases, warranties on products might become void if you don't follow recommendations. The following is general cleaning advice.

BUTCHER BLOCK COUNTERTOP

Clean with a mild soap and water. Wipe the butcher block dry immediately after cleaning.

Caution Don't allow water to sit on a butcher block countertop, because it will cause the surface to turn black.

CERAMIC FLOORING

Mop ceramic floors with water. Follow with a dry cloth to buff the floors and restore the shine.

Caution Never use an abrasive scrub, since it will dull the shine and wear down the surface colours.

CONCRETE COUNTERTOP

Mix a neutral cleaner with warm water. Clean with a soft cloth.

Caution Don't use abrasive cleaners or pads.

CONCRETE FLOOR

Vacuum with a brush attachment, working from left to right and from the far corner out. Wet the mop using all-purpose cleaner and water. Wipe back and forth toward the doorway. Rinse out and clean the mop frequently.

Caution Don't use abrasive cleaners and bleach products on concrete—they may damage the finish.

CORK FLOORING

Sweep or vacuum as needed, then damp-mop with a neutral floor cleaner.

Caution Never wet-mop or flood a cork floor.

GRANITE COUNTERTOP

Clean granite with a mild detergent and a damp sponge or cloth.

Caution Never use anything abrasive on a granite countertop, including a scrubby or scrub pad. Avoid products such as bleach, oil, vinegar, and ammonia that leave a residue.

GRANITE FLOORING

Dry-dust granite with a mop. Vacuum using a floor nozzle attachment that won't scratch. Mop using a mild detergent and warm water.

Caution Ensure that all dirt is lifted from the floor when mopping, because any remaining dirt will sink into the floor as the surface dries. The floor scratches easily, so clean carefully.

HARDWOOD FLOORING

Dry-mop or vacuum using the proper floor attachment. Use a damp mop to clean the floor. Buff dry.

Caution Do not wet-mop. Do not use furniture polish.

LAMINATE COUNTERTOP

Clean with a mild detergent applied with a soft cloth. Cover stubborn stains with a paste of baking soda and water (three parts baking soda to one part water) and leave for five to ten minutes. Clean off with a soft-bristled brush.

Caution Avoid using abrasive pads, scouring pads, or cleaners that will permanently dull the surface. Never allow water to stand on the countertop because it will seep through the seams, causing damage below.

LAMINATE FLOORING

Use a dust mop or vacuum with the hard floor attachment. Use a damp/almost-dry mop to clean the floor.

Caution Don't use excessive amounts of water or cleaner on laminate flooring. And don't use soap or detergent-based cleaners, abrasives, or ammonia. Avoid oil-based detergent, vinegar, and household cleaners because they'll dull the surface.

LINOLEUM FLOORING

Vacuum with the appropriate floor brush attachment. Damp-mop with a mixture of water and 1 capful to ¼ cup (50 mL) of concentrated all-purpose cleaner (check the product directions for recommended ratio). Be sure to rinse thoroughly after cleaning.

LIMESTONE COUNTERTOP

Use a soft cloth and a mild detergent to clean limestone countertops.

Caution Don't use bleach, oil, vinegar, ammonia, or products that leave a residue.

MARBLE COUNTERTOP

Use a neutral cleaner and a fresh clean cloth that hasn't been used to clean any other surface.

Caution Marble stains easily. Don't use abrasive cleaners on marble. Avoid bleach, oil, vinegar, lemon, ammonia, or other products that leave a residue.

MARBLE FLOORING

Clean with a dry dust mop before wet-mopping. Use a clean mop or cloth that's free of any chemicals or dirt because it may scratch the floor. Marble is prone to staining, so make sure to use a mild non-abrasive cleaner. Marble may also be cleaned with a minimal amount of warm clear water.

Caution Make sure to wipe up spilled liquids or foods immediately, or they may mar the finish. Don't use products that contain lemon, vinegar, or other acidic ingredients on marble flours. And don't use scouring pads, powders, or creams.

PAINTED WALLS

Always check the paint can for cleaning instructions, or contact the manufacturer or paint supplier. Otherwise, dust walls carefully, then clean washable paint finishes with a damp cloth and mild detergent. To remove stains, mix a thick paste of baking soda and water (three parts baking soda to one part water). Apply paste with a cloth and gently rub the stain away. And make sure to test this remedy in an inconspicuous area before trying it on a visible portion of your walls.

Caution Commercial spot removers may damage some paint surfaces.

QUARTZ (SILESTONE) COUNTERTOP

Clean quartz countertops with soapy water. Use abrasive soap carefully for stubborn stains.

Caution Oven cleaner will damage this surface if left on the countertop.

SLATE FLOORING

Wash with soapy water (a few squirts of dish detergent in water). Rinse well. Slate isn't damaged by alkali cleaners, but strong solutions aren't necessary.

SOAPSTONE COUNTERTOP

Use a neutral cleaner and a clean fresh cloth that hasn't been used to clean any other surface.

Caution Soapstone stains easily. Don't use abrasive cleaners on soapstone. And avoid bleach, oil, vinegars, ammonia, or products that will leave a residue.

SOLID SURFACE SYNTHETIC (CORIAN) COUNTERTOP

This is a synthetic material that resembles marble or granite. It has a non-porous surface. Clean with a mild detergent and water.

Caution This is a durable material, but in a counter, it can scratch. Use care when moving items on the countertop to avoid scratches.

STAINLESS STEEL COUNTERTOP

Use a soft cloth and a non-abrasive cleaner, such as all-purpose cleaner. Wipe in the direction of the grain.

Caution Stainless steel is easily scratched, so don't use abrasive pads or abrasive cleaners. Be careful with rings and bracelets, too.

SWITCHPLATES

Use a damp cloth and all-purpose cleaner, degreaser, or disinfectant to clean. Use cotton swabs dipped in cleaner to clean away grime around the switches.

TERRAZZO FLOORING

Damp-mop using all-purpose cleaner mixed with water. Use a separate mop or fresh cloth that's free of any chemicals or dirt—it may scratch the floor.

Caution Don't use acidic or alkali cleaners, since they'll damage the surface.

TILE COUNTERTOP

Use a non-abrasive cleaner, soft cloth, and warm water to clean tile.

Caution Be careful, because too much water can fall into the cracks and stain the grout.

TILE FLOORING

Vacuum periodically to remove dirt particles and dust. Wash the floor using all-purpose cleaner mixed with water. Let it dry.

VINYL FLOORING

Damp-mop with a mixture of water and 1 capful to ¼ cup (50 mL) of concentrated all-purpose cleaner (check the product directions for recommended ratio). Be sure to rinse thoroughly after cleaning.

WALLPAPERED WALLS

Depending on the type of wallpaper (vinyl and other treated wallpapers are washable), dust first, then wash with damp cloth.

WINDOWS

Spray glass cleaner sparingly onto the surface. Using a clean microfibre cloth, fold the cloth into four (so that there are actually eight surfaces for cleaning). Quickly wipe the window and then allow it to dry. If needed, polish and dry the glass surface with a clean, dry section of the cloth. Don't spray exterior windows if the outside temperature is below freezing, and don't spray windows that are hot from direct sunlight. For large areas, you can use a window squeegee. To eliminate streaks easily, wipe one side of the glass horizontally and the other side vertically. That way, when polishing out streaks, it'll be easy to determine which side they're on.

WOOD FLOORING

Dust, mop, or vacuum regularly. Dry-mop to clean. There shouldn't be any streaks—but if there are, be sure to dry them with a clean cloth.

Cleaning the Floor

Prepare any floor for cleaning by removing small items such as garbage cans, door mats, bath rugs, and so on. Use a vacuum or broom to pick up crumbs, loose dirt, and dust. Then wash the floor in 3-foot by 3-foot (1 m by 1 m) squares, overlapping the previously cleaned squares by 6 inches (15 cm). Use a damp cloth to wipe baseboards, corners, and dried-on food stains. Rinse the mop frequently. Depending on the type of floor it is, you may or may not have to buff dry.

KEEPING GREEN FLOORS CLEAN

The newest environmentally friendly floors are easy to keep clean.

* Clean bamboo floors with a dust mop.
* Clean reclaimed wood floors with a damp mop.
* Clean recycled glass tiles with a damp mop.

Solving Your Floor Problems

Here's a quick guide to solving common floor-cleaning problems.

PROBLEM	WHAT TO DO
Floors are dull	This usually happens because dirt or a cleaning product has accumulated on the floor. Clean the floor a few times with plain water.
Sticky floor	It's important to determine why floors are sticky. It could be the flooring material itself, so make sure to check with the flooring company or manufacturer. Perhaps you've used the wrong cleaning product. Sometimes floors are sticky because they haven't been rinsed properly. To remedy, thoroughly clean the floor using plain water. Change the water and repeat. Buff dry.
Stuck-on dirt	Sometimes gum, wax, and tar turn into hard-to-remove mounds on your floor. One easy way to get this off is to harden the lump with ice. Cover with ice or an ice tray for several minutes. When the lump freezes, chip it off immediately.
Scratches	Ask your local hardware store for advice about temporary fixes such as paste wax or wax-type pencils that fill in fine or small scratches. For permanent solutions, you may have to hire a professional.

The Lowdown on Carpets

Taking care of carpets will help to prolong their life. Here's how.

* Vacuum carpets regularly to remove dirt and dust and to keep them at their best.

* Vacuum carpets at least once a week, and more often if necessary in busy traffic areas such as hallways. Be sure to use the crevice tool for cleaning baseboards and radiators and other hard-to-reach places.

* Vacuum wall-to-wall carpeting systematically, moving from left to right and dividing the carpet into sections. Vacuum an entire section before moving on to the next.

* Vacuum plush carpets slowly, because dirt can be deeply embedded. Run the vacuum back and forth over an area several times—that way you'll be sure you're picking up everything.

* Use door mats to encourage family and guests to wipe their shoes. It's also a good idea to ask everyone to remove outdoor footwear at the door.

* When vacuuming, take extra time in the places where people sit and leave behind dirt and crumbs—in front of chairs and couches, and under tables. Criss-cross and overlap when you vacuum these spots.

* Soil-retardant products are available for new carpets or newly cleaned carpets. Discuss this with a manufacturer or professional carpet cleaner.

* Add a little baking soda to the vacuum bag to help fight odours.

* Move furniture slightly to avoid deeply flattened pile areas. Spraying the carpet with a light mist of water and fluffing its fibres will help to renew flattened areas.

* Air out rugs when possible. Hang them over a railing and beat out the dust. Leave rugs outside to air.

* Consider turning rugs occasionally in order to even out the wear and any fading caused by sunlight.

* Dark shades hide wear in carpets better than light shades, so choose darker shades if possible for heavy traffic areas.

* Have valuable wool and silk rugs professionally cleaned.

Spots and Spills on Carpets

When cleaning spots and spills on carpets, it's most important to treat the problem right away. Catching a fresh spill gives you the best chance of removing it. Here are some how-to tips.

* Blot or scrape a spill to remove as much of the material as possible.

* Before using a cleaning solution, test the carpet in a hidden spot to make sure the cleaner won't damage or discolour it.

* Never rub the spill—this may cause it to spread.

* Apply spot cleaner from the outside of the stain toward the inside. Blot up moisture.

* Use a clean lint-free cloth to dry carpet.

Do You Need to Deep Clean Carpets?

Here's a quick checklist to determine if it's time to clean your carpets.

❑ The surface feels dirty, sticky, or matted.

❑ The colour is much darker than it used to be.

❑ There are wear patterns in front of sofas and around chairs.

❑ When you walk across the carpet, you can see the dust.

If these descriptions fit your carpet, it needs a deep clean. Contact a professional carpet cleaner, or clean it yourself with a carpet cleaner. Here's a general guide.

* Test for colourfastness.

* Remove as much furniture from the room as possible, and place foil or plastic film under the legs and bases of the remaining furniture to prevent stains.

* Vacuum the carpet thoroughly, then spot clean and pre-treat stains before shampooing the carpet.

* Follow the instructions for the carpet cleaner.

* Use single strokes over the carpet surface.

* Don't apply heavy pressure with the machine.

* Wipe cleaning solutions and foam from furniture legs and woodwork immediately to prevent damage.

* Make sure the room is well ventilated after cleaning to speed drying.

* Avoid walking on carpets until they're completely dry.

11
Body Wise: Healthy Cleaning Solutions

Cleaning house is a highly physical activity, and it's important to protect yourself from injury, muscular aches and pains, and overuse injuries. There are obvious strategies. For example, never lift or move any object that's too heavy for one person, such as a fridge or big couch. There are less obvious strategies, too. For example, it's important to change your working arm frequently throughout the day. When you do this, you're letting the muscles in your body take turns at being used—and lowering the risk of an overuse injury. At the same time, the very nature of cleaning puts you in harm's way when it comes to germs, and there are different cleaning and hygiene habits that will keep you safe in that regard as well.

Can Cleaning Cause a Repetitive Stress Injury?

Unfortunately, it can. A repetitive stress injury is an injury to a part of your body caused by overusing or exerting too much stress on that body part. A good example of a chore that might cause a repetitive stress injury is washing windows for several hours with your right arm. By doing this you repeatedly stress the joints, muscles, and soft tissues in that arm. It's the repetition that causes the damage.

"Repetitive stress injury" is actually a large group of health-related conditions that can occur when you repeatedly do something that isn't comfortable. These conditions are often focused on a joint and affect the muscle, bone, or tendon of that joint. If your doctor has ever talked to you about carpal tunnel syndrome, tendonitis, bursitis, or tennis elbow, he or she is talking about a repetitive stress injury.

Enter ergonomics, which by definition is the science of work, or making your work both comfortable (keeping you safe and reducing the risk of repetitive stress injury) and efficient (getting the job done).

Here are ergonomic solutions to moves that can lead to injury when you're cleaning the house.

RISKY MOVE	ERGONOMIC SOLUTION
Kneeling on a hard surface with both knees, which puts a lot of pressure on knees.	Kneepads can reduce the pressure on your knees if you have to kneel down. If possible, kneel on just one knee and switch knees regularly to minimize and disperse pressure.
Bending over while you're standing, which is tough on your back.	Bend at the knees, not at the back, to bring yourself as close to your task as you can.
Over-reaching, which strains shoulders.	Get closer to your chore by using a stool, a stepladder, or an extendable cleaning tool.
Lying down when you're finished cleaning.	It's important to stretch the muscles you've been working.

Safe Cleaning Techniques

VACUUMING

* Carry the vacuum cleaner close to your body with a firm grip on the middle section.
* When vacuuming, walk the vacuum cleaner rather than lifting it around.
* Always hold the cord in one hand and keep the work close to your body.
* As you clean across a sofa, put your knee on the sofa for support.
* Keep the vacuum close to your body as you clean so that you're never overstretching.

MOVING FURNITURE

* If there's a carpeted floor and the furniture you're moving is lightweight (not a monstrous heavy sofa), move it by bending your knees and pushing or pulling.
* Never try to move heavy furniture and appliances by yourself.

GENERAL CLEANING

* It's hard work to wash a floor, wall, or shower stall. To protect yourself, alternate the cloth between your left and right hands.
* Alternate sweeping and mopping floors between your right and left sides, too.
* Always use a long-handled mop or stepstool to reach high spots you're cleaning rather than standing on counters, bathroom vanities, and the side of the bathtub.
* Never bend forward from the waist while you're standing to reach something on the floor. Instead, bend or kneel down to rinse out your cloth, for example. And kneel on one knee if possible, since kneeling down on both knees can sometimes put too much pressure on your knees.

Preventing Accidents

You probably know people who ended up in the hospital's emergency department because they slipped or fell while working around the house. It happens all the time, and that's why accident prevention is something we all need to think about. Most of us keep watch over children, toddlers, and aging parents, but it's important to also consider your own safety—and vulnerability—when you're cleaning.

Here are ways to accident-proof your home with cleaning in mind.

* Use anti-skid strips on the floor in the shower and bathtub.

* Put anti-slip backing on throw rugs.

* Repair or replace loose or frayed carpeting.

* Never leave toys or loose items on stairs or in hallways.

* Don't insist on carrying everything at the same time, whether you're emptying groceries from the car or putting away the pile of clothing and cleaning products sitting at the bottom of the stairs. Make two or three trips if you have to.

* Make sure freshly mopped floors are dry before you walk across them.

* Use a CSA-approved ladder when you need to reach up high. Don't use a box or chair. And while on the ladder, make sure you don't reach too far out. It's better to move the ladder than end up in the hospital's emergency room.

Safe Snow Removal

Winter brings its own set of cleaning hazards, the most significant being clearing snow from the paths around your home. Here's a guide to this heavy chore. It's good exercise, but it's important to make it a safe exercise. Here's how.

* Make sure your doctor has given you the thumbs-up for snow shovel-ling. (If it's a no-go, consider hiring a student or using a volunteer service.)

* Before starting to clear the path, warm up all the muscles in your body by walking or marching in place for several minutes.

* Always start slowly and work at a slow pace. Shovel for a few minutes, then rest for a few minutes.

* Remember to drink lots of water to prevent dehydration.

* The rule of thumb is to shovel early and often. Clear as much snow as you can when it's new and light.

* Use a good lightweight, sturdy shovel. Ergonomically correct models (with curved handles) will help prevent injury and fatigue.

HOW TO SHOVEL SNOW SAFELY

* Try to push snow rather than lifting it.

* When you lift snow, be sure to lift it properly to protect your back:

  * stand with feet at hip width for balance

  * hold the shovel close to your body

  * space hands apart to increase leverage

  * bend from your knees, not your back

  * tighten your stomach muscles while lifting

  * avoid twisting while lifting

  * walk to dump snow rather than throwing it.

* If snow is deep, shovel small amounts (1–2 inches/2–5 cm) at a time.

* If the ground is icy or slippery, spread an environmentally friendly de-icer product, salt, sand, or kitty litter to create better foot traction.

* Listen to your body. Stop shovelling if you experience any suspicious symptoms such as sudden shortness of breath, discomfort in the chest, light-headedness, nausea, dizziness, or severe headache.

Germs in the Home

Did you know that regular cleaning of floors and surfaces as well as washing hands are the simplest ways to lower the risk of spreading germs?

Door handles, telephones, and keyboards in particular are some of the biggest culprits in transferring germs. We all learn to cover our mouths when we cough—but when we cough into our hands, we cover them with germs and transfer those germs to everything we touch.

The Public Health Agency of Canada says that hands spread an estimated eighty percent of common diseases such as the common cold and flu. For example, when you touch a doorknob that has a flu virus on it and then touch your mouth, chances are you may get sick.

The solution is very simple: Wash your hands. Rubbing your hands together with soap and water helps to break down the bits of grease, fat, and dirt on your hands that germs cling to. The combination of soaping, rubbing, rinsing, and drying helps these bugs slide off your hands.

HOW TO WASH YOUR HANDS

* Remove rings. Wet hands under warm running water.
* Use a small amount of liquid soap in the palm of one hand.
* Rub hands together and lather up soap for twenty seconds. Scrub between fingers, under nails if possible, and over the backs of hands.
* Rinse hands with clean running water for at least ten seconds. Try not to touch faucets once hands are clean. Use a paper towel to turn off water.
* Dry hands with a single-use paper towel. If there's a hand towel in the washroom, be sure to change it daily. During cold and flu season, give each family member his or her own hand towel.
* Teach children how to wash their hands, too!

Where Do Germs Hide in the House?

The Public Health Agency of Canada reports that if you had to choose the place in your house with the most disease-causing germs, many people would automatically think of the toilet seat or bathroom floor. In fact, the kitchen is the biggest hot spot for disease-causing germs, with the top prize going to the kitchen sink, followed by the sink dishcloth or sponge.

Germs can also live for a long time on hard surfaces such as desks, doorknobs, and tables. Most people get sick when they touch something that's contaminated with germs and then touch their eyes, nose, or mouth. Here's a germ warfare list for the home.

1. Teach everyone to wash hands often, using soap and water.

2. Keep the kitchen sink and counters clean.

3. Disinfect the bathroom—and don't forget the doorknobs and faucet.

4. Regularly disinfect your desk and keyboard.

5. Don't share mugs, cups, or pens.

6. Don't use sponges for cleaning. Use dishcloths, and make sure to launder them every day.

Exercise and Cleaning: What a Pair!

Anyone who questions whether cleaning is real exercise has never washed floors and walls for a day. It's real exercise and helps keep you strong and healthy. Here are Body Wise recommendations to keep in mind while you're "exercising" in the home.

Remember your posture Try not to slouch when you work because it tires out your body faster. Keep shoulders square and relaxed, chest proud, and stomach in.

Take five-minute breaks Throughout your busy day, take a timeout and stay hydrated by drinking water, juice, or a decaffeinated beverage.

Tune in and "whistle while you work" Playing music, singing, whistling, and humming all make your work more fun. Turn up the volume and sing to your heart's content.

Skip the gym today When you move your body, you're exercising. Feel good about all the exercise you're doing when you clean your house.

Count on burning calories All that cleaning is burning calories, too. Fifteen minutes of vacuuming burns around eighty calories. Wash out the shower, mop the floor, and wipe fingerprints from doors and switchplates. You're getting a pretty good workout—and a cleaner house.

No stationary equipment for you! Gym members spend a lot of time on treadmills and stair machines, but guess what? You're doing the same exercise (walking around the house and going up and down the stairs), only you're getting housecleaning done at the same time.

Comfort comes first Be sure to wear comfortable clothing that allows you to move easily when you're cleaning. Housework involves a lot of twisting, turning, and slopping things about.

It's a "shoe"-in Always wear good supportive shoes that protect your feet and prevent accidents, rather than lightweight slippers or stocking feet.

Stretch

It's a good idea to stretch the muscle groups you're working while you clean. Take a stretch break a few times throughout your cleaning day, and always stretch when you're finished. Repeat these stretches up to five times.

Stretch your back A back extension stretch will feel great after you've been cleaning in a forward position. Stand with your feet shoulder-width apart. Put your hands on your lower back (just above the buttocks). Look straight ahead and slowly lean back until you feel a slight stretch in your back muscles. Enjoy the feeling. Return slowly to your upright standing starting position.

Cat stretch Here's another stretch for your back and upper shoulders. Kneel on your hands and knees (with hips over knees and shoulders over wrists). Pull your navel up toward your spine and round your back up (like a cat). Hold for five seconds. Return to your starting position.

Chest opener (and shoulder stretch) Sit or stand and clasp your hands together behind your back. Holding your hands or fingers, open your chest by pulling your shoulder blades together. Lift your arms up behind you slightly if you can. Hold for a few seconds.

Neck stretch Sit or stand. Press your shoulders down and drop your right ear toward your right shoulder. Feel the stretch from the area behind the left ear to the tip of the left shoulder. Hold for a few seconds. Change sides.

Upper arm/triceps stretch Hold one arm just above the elbow with the opposite hand. Gently pull your elbow toward your opposite shoulder. Hold the stretch for a few seconds. Change sides.

Finger fan With your arms relaxed at your sides, spread your fingers apart. Hold for five seconds and relax.

12
On-the-Spot Solutions

The first golden rule of stain removal is to deal with a stain right away. In fact, the more quickly you deal with it, the more likely you are to be successful. At the same time, when it comes to tackling stains, water should always be the first cleaner you try. Simply flush the area or material with cool water, mopping up as you go. If water doesn't work, here's an A to Z guide to common cleaning challenges around the house. Most of the cleaning products suggested here are already in your kitchen!

THE GOLDEN RULES OF STAIN REMOVAL

* Deal with a stain right away.
* Soak up excess liquid and scrape off excess solids.
* Dab—don't scrub.
* Use a white cotton cloth to dab the spot rather than using anything coloured (so that you don't add colour to the problem).
* Test for colourfastness in an inconspicuous area, if possible, before using any solvents.
* Use cool or warm water, never cold or hot.

ABSORBENT POWDERS

Using an absorbent powder is an important on-the-spot solution—and you can find several in your kitchen. A product such as salt, baking soda (sodium bicarbonate), or cornstarch can pick up wet stains or grease. How to deal with a stain: Sprinkle the absorbent powder liberally over the stain and leave it to dry. Then brush or vacuum the powder—and the stain—away. Repeat if necessary.

ADHESIVE TAPE

To remove stubborn adhesive tape, cover it with a wet cloth for a while. Then rinse and wash as usual.

ALUMINUM

Wash aluminum in warm soapy water and rub stains gently with fine steel wool, working in one direction only. If food spills are on the bottom of an aluminum pan, cover the spot with vinegar and add 1 tablespoon (15 mL) of salt. Let it soak overnight, and scrub the pan the next day.

BATHTUB

If staining in the bathtub is severe, rub toothpaste into the stain and leave it on for one to two days before rinsing off.

BIRD DROPPINGS

Scrape off what you can, then soak in a warm detergent solution. Rinse and wash again.

BLENDERS AND FOOD PROCESSORS

Follow the manufacturer's instructions for everyday cleaning. For stubborn residue, put 2 teaspoons (10 mL) of baking soda and ½ cup (125 mL) of vinegar into the bowl or jug, put the lid on, and turn on the machine for twenty seconds. Rinse.

BLINDS

Use a sponge dipped in mild soap and water. For stained roman blinds, sponge with a mild detergent. Alternatively, take them down and soak overnight in a towel-lined tub (to protect the tub from scratches), then rinse.

BLOOD

Rinse a blood stain in cold water as soon as possible. If the stain is on the carpet, apply cold water and blot with an absorbent cloth. If the blood has dried, brush off as much as possible, then treat with a solution of salt and lemon juice—or any type of soap with warm water—and rub into the stain. Once it has started to clear, wash in cold or warm water.

BONE HANDLES

Wash quickly in warm water and dry. Don't put ivory or bone-handled cutlery in the dishwasher—or wash in hot water at all—because it will discolour and may split.

BRASS

Clean with warm soapy water, and then polish with a commercial brass polish. Use a dry cloth to buff and shine. Alternatively, rub with a piece of lemon sprinkled with salt, then rinse and dry. To finish, rub with olive oil to remove polish and produce a shine.

BUTTER

On upholstery, carpet, or non-washable fabric, scrape as much butter off as you can, then place absorbent or brown paper on the mark and press with a warm iron. Keep an eye on it so that you don't damage the fabric.

CANDLE WAX

Scrape off as much of the hardened candle wax as possible. Place absorbent fabric or brown paper on both sides of the mark and press with a warm iron. If candleholders are coated with wax, put them in the freezer for an hour or so and the wax will peel off easily.

CANE FURNITURE

Dissolve 2 teaspoons (10 mL) of baking soda in 4 cups (1 L) of water. Dip a sponge into the mixture and rub the stain on the cane furniture. Rinse.

CARPET

Most carpets can be washed. Sponge with warm soapy water, then thoroughly rinse. For a fresh spill, sponge off the excess and saturate the stain with soda water. Sponge again. Saturate with baking soda and leave to dry. Vacuum.

CAST-IRON COOKWARE

To clean, wipe with a cloth dampened in hot water and a little detergent.

CERAMIC TILE

Clean with all-purpose cleaner on a damp cloth or mop. For resistant stains, sprinkle with baking soda before cleaning with a damp cloth or a mop.

CHANDELIER

Cover the floor and/or table with plastic and then newspaper or a towel in order to catch the drips. Turn off the light. When light bulbs are cool to the touch, immerse each pendant for a few seconds in a glass of hot water and vinegar (or put a mixture of hot water and vinegar into a spray bottle and spray the pendants). Allow to drip dry.

CHEWING GUM

If you find old chewing gum stuck to the carpet or couch, freeze with ice then chip and scrape away the pieces.

CHROME

Wash in warm soapy water. To polish, rub with baking soda on a dry cloth.

COPPER

Coated copper products can be cleaned with soap and water. To clean uncoated copper, use a paste of salt and lemon juice, rubbed on with a soft cloth. Rinse with water and dry.

CRAYON MARKS

Sponge crayon marks on walls or other flat surfaces with all-purpose cleaner.

DECANTERS

Clean narrow-necked glass containers such as decanters, carafes, and vases by filling them three-quarters full with hot water and adding 1 teaspoon (5 mL) baking soda. Shake well.

DISHES

To remove baked-on food from a cooking dish, fill it with boiling water, add 2 tablespoons (30 mL) baking soda or salt, and leave it to soak.

ENAMEL COOKWARE

If food is cooked on, fill the pan with water and 2 teaspoons (10 mL) of baking soda. Bring to a boil and leave to soak for at least a half-hour. Alternatively, soak the pan overnight in salted water. Bring to a boil the next day and scrub gently.

FAT

For fresh spots, blot as much as possible, then sprinkle and work in an absorbent powder such as cornstarch. Leave for a half-hour, then brush off. Repeat several times until the spot is removed.

FINGERPRINTS

Use water and dish soap with a soft cloth to spot-clean fingerprints off the walls.

FLOOR MATS

Vacuum regularly. Move the mat and vacuum underneath as well, if possible. For spills, apply a little soda water as soon as you can and let dry.

FLOORS

Clean most floors by mopping with warm water and all-purpose cleaner.

GREASE

In general, blot the stain, and then sprinkle with an absorbent powder such as cornstarch or baking soda. Work in and leave for a half-hour, then brush off. Repeat several times until the spot is removed.

GRILL

Wash grill in hot soapy water after every use. If marks are resistant, spray with a degreaser and scrub.

GROUT

The grout around tiles in kitchens and bathrooms is prone to staining and/or discolouration. To clean, wipe with a damp cloth, then sprinkle with baking soda and scrub with an old toothbrush.

HAIRSPRAY

Hot soapy water should remove stubborn hairspray marks from the mirror.

HEAT MARKS

On waxed or polished furniture, apply a paste of equal parts baking soda and olive oil and leave for a few minutes. Remove with a soft cloth.

LIGHT SWITCHES AND SWITCHPLATES

Wipe these surfaces with a degreaser applied to a cloth. Never spray any liquid on a light switch, since you may cause a short circuit.

MARBLE

Marble is easily damaged. Be sure to use a gentle neutral cleaner and a clean cloth. Don't use abrasive cleaners or bleach, oil, vinegar, ammonia, or other products that leave a residue.

MICROWAVE

To remove food splatters in a microwave, soften them first by filling a cup with water and microwaving it on high for one minute. The dirt will wipe off.

MUD

To remove mud stains on carpet, first remove any solids and allow mud to dry. Vacuum or sweep up as much as possible. Treat with liquid detergent, rubbing gently every few minutes. Sponge off with cold water.

ODOURS

Baking soda is a great absorber of smells. Put a handful into the bottom of your kitchen garbage. Place an open box in the fridge. Here are other natural air fresheners.

Vinegar with lemon juice in small dishes absorbs odours around the house. Houseplants help reduce odours in the home.

- Prevent cooking odours by simmering vinegar—1 tablespoon (15 mL) in 1 cup (250 mL) of water—on the stove while cooking.
- To get strong odours such as fish and onion from utensils and cutting boards, wipe with vinegar and wash in soapy water.
- Keep fresh coffee grounds on the counter.
- Grind up a slice of lemon in the garbage disposal.
- Simmer water and cinnamon or other spices on the stove.
- Place bowls of fragrant dried herbs and flowers in a room.

OIL

For fresh spots, blot as much as possible, then sprinkle and work in an absorbent powder such as cornstarch. Leave for a half-hour, then brush off. Repeat several times until the spot is removed.

POLLEN

To remove pollen stains on a carpet, use fresh pieces of sticky tape to lift them off. Or make sure they're totally dry and use a strong vacuum cleaner.

REFRIGERATOR

Remove spills from inside the refrigerator with a cloth and a solution of baking soda and warm water. Rinse with water.

SCUFF MARKS

Use a drop of baby oil to clean away scuff marks on the floor.

TOILET BOWL RINGS

Use a pumice stone to safely and easily remove these stains.

VINYL FLOOR

To remove stains and scuffs from a vinyl floor, rub with a paste of baking soda and water.

VOMIT

To remove vomit from a carpet or mattress, remove solid matter and use an old towel to blot up as much moisture as possible. Use a manufacturer-recommended carpet cleaner to remove any stains.

WINDOW TRACKS

Remove dirt from window tracks by spraying all-purpose cleaner into the tracks. It will lift dirt and make the window slide more easily.

WINE

To clean up a red wine spill on fabric, mop up the excess with a clean cloth or towel and rinse with soda water (dab, don't wipe).

Appendices

MOLLY MAID Q&A
Cleaning Checklist Compendium

MOLLY MAID
Q&A

Concerned about keeping your ivory piano keys clean? Wondering what advice to give your son for keeping his first-year dorm room tidy? Here we've assembled a miscellany of challenges, from tackling messy kitchen cupboards to opening up a long-unused cottage.

PERSNICKETY PROBLEMS

Grease

Q: How do you degrease a stovetop?

MM: First and foremost, it's important to get into the habit of cleaning grease splatters from the stovetop every time you cook. Fresh grease splatters are much easier to remove than hardened grease. Wet a microfibre cloth with warm soapy water and wring it out, then wipe the surface of the stove. If the grease has been sitting on the stovetop for a while, wet the spill first with a little warm water and then clean it up. For tougher, baked-on grease stains, use a degreaser product. Spray on the degreaser and let it sit for a few minutes. Then use a damp cloth to wipe away the grease. Make sure to clean any grease splatters off the wall and backsplash behind your stove as well. To reduce the amount of grease splattering on the stovetop and hood in the first place, use a mesh splatter screen over pots and pans while you're cooking. Ask about these screens at a specialty kitchen store or department store.

Dust Collectors

Q: What are the biggest dust collectors in a home … and what can I do about them?

MM: Sorry to say, but some of our favourite things can also be the biggest dust collectors—for example, knickknacks, stuffed animals sitting on shelves, even books. The solution isn't to get rid of these much-loved possessions, obviously, but to dust and clean them regularly. Of course, the more of these dust collectors you have, the more time it will take to clean them.

Salt and Hardwood Floors

Q: During the winter we tend to track in a lot of salt. We have hardwood floors and I'm wondering if salt is bad news.

MM: Yes, salt is definitely bad news because it's corrosive; think about how it eats through snow and ice. You don't want salt on your floors for long, so gently sweep up salt pieces right away. Wipe salt stains as soon as possible, too. Make sure to wash the floor with clear, clean water. Dry-mop to finish. And to prevent salt from getting inside in the first place, place a mat at the door to trap dirt and salt before it gets tracked in.

Unfinished Wood

Q: I have a lot of antique furniture. How can I clean the unfinished wood?

MM: Use a dry microfibre cloth to wipe away any dirt and debris from the surface. (Don't ever use water on unfinished wood because it can cause the fibres to swell and possibly splinter.) To protect the wood, use beeswax or linseed oil (available from a hardware or home supply store). Use the polish sparingly, and buff with a soft cloth, working along the grain.

Piano Keys

Q: How do I clean piano keys?

MM: Clean ivory piano keys by gently wiping them with a soft clean cloth that's been rinsed in soapy water. Make sure the cloth is squeezed almost dry. For the black keys, use a different damp cloth (also squeezed almost dry) and no soap. Give the piano keys a few minutes to air dry, then buff with a clean, lint-free microfibre cloth. And remember to keep the piano closed when it's not being used in order to protect the keys from dust and dirt.

Hair Dye

Q: My son splashed hair dye on the bathroom wall. How do I get that off?

MM: The key here is to try to clean up the stain as quickly as possible—so make sure to share this information with anyone in your family who's using hair dye. The best way to clean it is with soap and water and a clean microfibre cloth. If that doesn't work, or if the stain has been left too long, try rubbing it gently with a cotton ball dipped in rubbing alcohol. At the same time, it's important to know that, despite all your cleaning efforts, the stain may not come off because hair dye is such a strong substance.

ZONES OF ZEAL

Floors

Q: I don't have the time to clean my floors several times a day, but they're constantly getting dirty. Do you have tips for keeping them clean?

MM: Keeping floors dirt-free and clean is one of those chores that often need to be done once or twice a day. If you can, wipe up spills and dirt as they happen—because when spots dry, they're much harder to clean. Also, leaving the dirt only means it might be tracked through the house. To avoid this, get into the habit of sweeping or vacuuming the rooms that have the most traffic at least once a day—and more often if you have a busy household that includes kids and pets. When you clean up after dinner, for example, do the dishes, wipe the table, and sweep or vacuum the floor. Here's how to clean a floor:

- Vacuum or sweep the floor, starting in the corner farthest from the door.
- Soak a cloth in a bucket filled with hot water and all-purpose cleaner and wring it out. Wipe the baseboards and into the corners.
- Mop or wash the floor, making sure to rinse the mop or cloth often.
- If there are streaks, dry them with a clean cloth.
- Remember that mats at the front and back doors of the house will help to keep dirt out. Ask everyone to wipe shoes or remove them before coming inside. And shake out the mats regularly.

Carpets

Q: My carpets are worn and dirty, but we can't afford to replace them now. Do you have any cleaning and refreshing tips?

MM: Here are a few ideas:

- Start with deep-cleaning shampoo to get your carpets in the best shape they can be.
- Vacuum carpets regularly.
- Use a spot cleaner for the most visible spots. Ask at a home supply store or hardware store, and remember to test the product in an inconspicuous spot first in order to make sure it won't fade the carpet.
- Refresh carpets by sprinkling baking soda over them, letting it sit (to absorb odours), then vacuuming the baking soda up after several minutes.
- Buy another carpet or area rug with finished edges and put it on top of the worn carpet. This is a temporary solution, but it works.

Windows

Q: Windows are such a big job. How do I keep them clean?

MM: Windows should be on your Deep Clean list, and if there are smokers in your home or if you have a fireplace or wood-burning stove, you'll need to be extra diligent about cleaning your windows regularly. Also, certain rooms will require more regular window cleaning—for example, the kitchen, where cooking smells and grease settle on surfaces. To clean windows, use window cleaner, a clean microfibre cloth, and a little elbow grease. Spray the window cleaner on the surface. Polish dry with a clean, lint-free cloth. If you're cleaning both sides (of sliding doors, say), clean the glass by wiping horizontally on one side and vertically on the other so that you can see and avoid streaks. We recommend that you clean the entire window, but if you're not able to, just spot clean fingerprints when you see them. Although many windows are designed for ease of cleaning (they tilt in and come apart easily), for those tough-to-clean windows, especially the outside of windows, many people hire a professional window cleaning service once or twice a year.

Kitchen Cupboards

Q: The most-used cupboards in the kitchen are always the messiest. What advice do you have for keeping them clean?

MM: It's important to spend a few minutes every day tidying well-used cupboards and drawers. And make sure you aren't simply rearranging everything in the cupboard. Here are a few tips:

- Ask yourself, Do I use these items regularly? Are foods past their best-before date?

- When you go to the cupboard to grab the salt or pepper while you're cooking and you notice things are starting to look untidy, take a minute right there to sort things out. If you leave it, it will only get worse.

- Whenever you take something out of the cupboard, put it back in the same place.

- Maintain an organized cupboard in the first place so that it's obvious where each item should be. For example, you might group together all your Indian spices in a small basket. Other baking supplies should all go on the same shelf.

- If there isn't enough space for everything, declutter the cupboard by relocating the least-used items to the basement or the garage.

Front Hall Closet

Q: The front hall closet is always a disaster (there are six of us in the family). Any suggestions?

MM: Decluttering and cooperation are the main solutions—because there's no way six people in a house can fit all their coats and shoes (and hats, scarves, and gloves in the winter) in one closet. If possible, put up coat hooks near the front door and find alternative locations for various articles of clothing for everyone in the family. Ask everyone to help keep the closet clean by hanging things up properly and by taking some of the coats and shoes to other storage locations, such as individual rooms or a closet in the basement. And make sure to store off-season coats and footwear somewhere else.

Toilet

Q: What's the best way to keep the toilet bowl clean and fresh?

MM: Constant cleaning with bathroom cleaner and a toilet brush is the best way. In between cleans, you may be able to get the toilet itself to do some of the work. A toilet with a powerful flush can make a difference—so if you're in the market for a new toilet, do a flush test before you buy it. Many retailers have toilets hooked up to water so that you can see for yourself. Even newer high-efficiency toilets that use less water can provide a powerful flush … and that flush helps keep the toilet bowl clean.

TIME AND THE SEASONS

No Time to Clean

Q: My husband and I work full-time and are busy taking care of our three kids when we're home. It seems there's never any time to clean. What can we do to keep our house clean?

MM: Finding time to clean is really hard for many of us today. Sometimes it's best to lower your expectations and use the time you do have for rooms that are most important to keep clean—the high-traffic kitchen, bathroom, and family room. You could also decide to focus on one room once a week. For example, on Tuesdays after dinner, spend a half-hour cleaning the kitchen; on Thursdays before bed, spend a half-hour cleaning the bathrooms; and on Saturdays before weekend outings and activities start, spend time cleaning the family room. Lighten the load by getting everyone in the family to help. Here are a few more tricks.

Always keep your eyes open for what needs to be cleaned—and clean it when you can. This means you'll be multi-tasking a lot—for example, tidying up the kitchen while you oversee the kids doing their homework at the kitchen table, putting things in their place as you walk downstairs to get breakfast, sweeping the floor while you're defrosting dinner in the microwave, or wiping out the bathroom sink while you're filling the bathtub for a much-deserved soak.

Do the small jobs that need to be done often rather than letting chores build up. That's when you start to feel you'll never get everything done.

If you like to relax in front of the television, sneak in chores during commercial breaks. There are lots of thirty-second chores you can do: folding laundry, collecting garbage throughout the house, or unloading the dishwasher.

Robot Cleaners

Q: I've seen a battery-operated robot-type floor cleaner. Do you recommend using these types of helpers in the home?

MM: Anything that helps you keep your house clean is a good idea, but a battery-operated robot-type floor cleaner is a little gimmicky, and it can't replace a real person with a vacuum or broom. If you like this kind of thing, go for it—but be sure to keep a vacuum and broom handy, too.

Cleaning Day

Q: Do you recommend scheduled cleaning days?

MM: Yes. Like anything else, if you don't schedule a chore or activity, it's not likely to happen. When you're busy, it's easy to put cleaning off and say you'll do it tomorrow. But having a scheduled cleaning day, whether on the weekend or during the week, will help you get into the cleaning routine. Once cleaning day becomes a habit, you'll do it without even thinking.

Cleaning Checklists

Q: What's the best way to use cleaning checklists in each room?

MM: Having a pre-determined list of cleaning chores in each room is a good idea because it will help you get everything you want done, done. Also, many people get a sense of accomplishment from checking off chores on a cleaning list. Make copies of the checklist and keep track of the various chores. Alternatively, get one copy laminated at a business supply store and use a washable marker to check off all the various chores. Then wash it off and start fresh next cleaning day.

Spring Cleaning

Q: Is spring cleaning still necessary?

MM: Absolutely! Spring cleaning is generally regarded as cleaning a house thoroughly at the end of winter, and traditionally this is a great time to do this type of clean—following several months of cold weather and closed-up homes. But a thorough clean is recommended in the fall as well, because dust and pollen have built up and many people have run their air conditioning for much of the summer.

The Cottage

Q: We're reopening a cottage that has been closed for a few years. How do we tackle a project this big?

MM: This is a great spring project for your whole family. In preparation, go in and assess what needs to be cleaned (such as floors, the kitchen, the bathroom). Keep in mind that you'll need to load up on cleaning products and cloths—and you'll likely need more than usual, since this is such a big job. Dust is going to be your biggest problem, so be sure to open up all the windows to air out the cottage. Also, it'll be important to change the rinse water more than usual as you clean. Before you start, you might sort through each room to determine what you want to keep, what can be given to charity, and what might be good for a garage sale. Then, follow the MOLLY MAID cleaning rule: Clean each room from top to bottom, left to right. Divide the chores and cleaning products and get to work. As prevention for next year, be sure to clean the cottage thoroughly when you close it up in the fall—that will save you a lot of work.

University Life

Q: My son is heading off to university in the fall. How can I help him keep his dorm room clean?

MM: Remember the saying "A place for everything and everything in its place"? Well, the key to keeping a small dorm room clean is to be organized—so what you can do is help your son organize his stuff when he gets there and suggest he keep things as tidy as he can. One way to help him do this is to go shopping for organizational containers of different kinds. Remind him to remove dishes and garbage constantly, and not to let chip bags and banana peels pile up in the corner. (Another saying, after all, is "*Dormitory* is an anagram for *dirty room*." But let's not dwell.) Tell him also to keep a hamper for dirty clothes, and to put everything back where it belongs.

First Apartment

Q: What's a great first apartment-cleaning gift for my twenty-five-year-old daughter?

MM: Here are two suggestions.

- A good vacuum cleaner with tools on board (so she won't lose tools) and a HEPA filter.
- A collection of cleaning products in a bucket with a microfibre cloth.

ENVIRONMENTALLY SPEAKING

Identifying the Products

Q: How do you know a cleaning product is safe for the environment as well as for family and pets?

MM: Bio-based cleaning products are labelled as such and often include the following descriptions on the label: phosphate-free, low-phosphate, chlorine-free, non-toxic, bio-based, environmentally preferable, and biodegradable.

Justifying the Time

Q: Sometimes cleaning the environmental way takes more time and effort. How do I justify that extra work and time when I'm so busy in the rest of my life?

MM: Cleaning the environmental way is a commitment you've made to help the environment and to make your own environment healthier for you—keep that in mind when you clean. It's true that using bio-based cleaning products means you may have to change the way you clean, because sometimes these products can take a bit longer to help you do the job. But all that really means is approaching chores differently, perhaps by multi-tasking a little while you wait for the cleaner to work. For example, after spraying the shower with washroom cleaner, wipe out the sink while the cleaning product does its job. Return to the shower after five minutes, and wipe as usual.

Cleaning Checklist Compendium

Here, in one handy place, we've put together all the end-of-chapter, room-by-room checklists in the book.

Bathroom Cleaning Schedule Checklist

EVERYDAY CLEAN

❏ Declutter.

❏ Wipe out sink.

❏ Wipe tap handles and faucet.

❏ Fold up towels.

❏ Keep toilet bowl clean.

❏ Squeegee walls/shower door after showers.

CLEANING DAY

❏ Shake out/clean bath rugs.

❏ Dust ceiling, windowsills, and baseboards.

❏ Clean vanity.

❏ Wipe walls, doors.

❏ Clean the toilet.

❏ Clean and polish sink, shower, and tub.

❑ Clean, dry, and shine all mirrors, chrome, and tile.

❑ Collect/empty trash.

❑ Change bath towels.

❑ Vacuum/sweep floor.

❑ Wash floor.

DEEP CLEAN

❑ Launder bath rugs.

❑ Clean out cupboards and drawers.

❑ Clean the fan.

❑ Clean the medicine chest.

❑ Wash shower curtain and liner.

❑ Wash windows and window coverings.

❑ Deep clean lighting fixtures.

❑ Scrub bathtub slip mat.

Kitchen Cleaning Schedule Checklist

EVERYDAY CLEAN

❏ Declutter.

❏ Wipe up spills.

❏ Clear dirty dishes.

❏ Put away food.

❏ Wipe counters and the kitchen table.

❏ Wipe out sink.

❏ Keep garbage and compost containers clean.

❏ Change kitchen dishcloth.

❏ Sweep kitchen floor.

CLEANING DAY

❑ Shake out mats and/or rugs.

❑ Dust ceilings and windowsills.

❑ Clean, dry, and shine all appliance surfaces, range hood, and sink.

❑ Clean stove drip pans, burner grates, and control knobs.

❑ Clean the microwave oven inside and out, including the turntable.

❑ Clean the fridge, wiping shelves and the door rim, where mould often develops.

❑ Wash countertops.

❑ Damp wipe cupboard fronts, table, and chairs.

❑ Compost or discard old food.

❑ Check if windows and other glass surfaces in the kitchen need to be washed.

❑ Clean compost bucket and garbage can.

❑ Clean pet's eating area.

❑ Collect/empty trash.

❑ Vacuum/sweep floor.

❑ Wash floor.

DEEP CLEAN

- ❏ Clean under and behind appliances.

- ❏ Clean closets, cupboards, and drawers.

- ❏ Clean curtains, other window coverings, and windows.

- ❏ Compost or discard old food.

- ❏ Clean the oven, including racks.

- ❏ Degrease the stove's hood.

- ❏ Clean refrigerator condenser coils.

- ❏ Defrost the freezer.

- ❏ Deep clean small appliances.

- ❏ Clean out pantry and fridge.

Bedroom Cleaning Schedule Checklist

EVERYDAY CLEAN

❑ Declutter.

❑ Make bed (everyone is responsible for his or her own).

❑ Put clothes away.

❑ Put dirty laundry in hamper.

CLEANING DAY

❑ Shake out scatter rugs.

❑ Change bed linens.

❑ Collect/empty trash.

❑ Dust the ceiling and corners.

❑ Dust behind doors, under dressers, desks, and bed.

❑ Dust and clean all surfaces.

❑ Clean surfaces, including windowsills and frames, doors and switch-plates with a damp cloth.

❑ Clean windows, tracks, and mirrors.

❑ Vacuum and/or wash the floor.

DEEP CLEAN

- ❑ Clean windows and tracks.

- ❑ Turn the mattress at least twice a year.

- ❑ Launder the mattress cover.

- ❑ Clean the bedskirt.

- ❑ Vacuum the mattress.

- ❑ Replace pillow covers.

- ❑ Wash duvets.

- ❑ Wash the valance.

- ❑ Launder or dry clean curtains.

- ❑ Sort through your wardrobe and drawers.

- ❑ Clean blankets, duvets, and pillows.

- ❑ Polish frames of pictures and mirrors.

- ❑ Shampoo carpet.

Living Room / Dining Room
Family Room
Cleaning Schedule Checklist

EVERYDAY CLEAN

❑ Declutter.

❑ Wipe up spills.

❑ Clean up after pets.

❑ Clear off table.

❑ Sweep floor.

CLEANING DAY

❑ Dust ceilings, walls, and windowsills.

❑ Dust behind doors, under tables, and other furniture.

❑ Dust and clean all surfaces, including windowsills and frames, doors and switchplates.

❑ Dry-dust stereo, TV, and other electronics.

❑ Clean dining room table.

❑ Vacuum carpets, stairs, and upholstery.

- ❏ Clean lamps.

- ❏ Clean windows and mirrors.

- ❏ Sweep or vacuum.

- ❏ Wash floor.

DEEP CLEAN

- ❏ Clean under furniture.

- ❏ Shampoo carpets and upholstery.

- ❏ Clean out cabinets and drawers.

- ❏ Clean curtains and other window coverings.

- ❏ Deep clean lighting fixtures.

- ❏ Dust and clean books.

- ❏ Polish wooden furniture.

- ❏ Polish frames of mirrors and pictures.

- ❏ Clean (and reverse) ceiling fan blades.

Home Office Cleaning Schedule Checklist

EVERYDAY CLEAN

❑ Declutter.

❑ Wipe up spills.

❑ Sort garbage.

❑ Leave desk tidy.

CLEANING DAY

❑ Dust ceilings and walls.

❑ Shake out and dust curtains and other window coverings.

❑ Dust and clean all surfaces.

❑ Collect/empty trash.

❑ Wipe off telephones.

❑ Clean and buff surfaces (mirrors, windows).

❑ Clean lamps.

❑ Clean office equipment.

❑ Wipe office chair.

- ❏ Vacuum carpets, rugs, and stairs.

- ❏ Vacuum or sweep bare floors.

- ❏ Wash floor.

DEEP CLEAN

- ❏ Dust and wash all surfaces.

- ❏ Clean under furniture.

- ❏ Shampoo carpets and upholstery.

- ❏ Clean out filing cabinets and other office storage.

- ❏ Clean curtains and other window coverings.

- ❏ Deep clean lighting fixtures.

- ❏ Dust and clean books.

Laundry Room
Cleaning Schedule Checklist

EVERYDAY CLEAN

❑ Declutter.

❑ Wipe up all spills immediately.

❑ Sort and wash laundry ongoing.

❑ Fold and put away clothes.

❑ Clean out dryer lint trap.

CLEANING DAY

❑ Shake out scatter rugs/mats.

❑ Wipe appliances down.

❑ Clean insides of appliances.

❑ Clean folding table and other surfaces.

❑ Collect/empty trash.

❑ Sweep or vacuum floor.

❑ Wash floor.

DEEP CLEAN

☐ Dust ceiling down to floor.

☐ Wipe out hampers.

☐ Clean laundry bags.

☐ Clean behind washer and dryer.

☐ Repaint floor if cement.

☐ Clean products shelf or drawer.

☐ Clean out storage.

While you're in the basement:

☐ Check batteries in smoke detectors (annual).

☐ Change furnace filter (as per manufacturer's recommendations).

☐ Professional maintenance of heating/cooling units (annual).

Pets in Your Home Cleaning Schedule Checklist

EVERYDAY CLEAN

❑ Pick up after pets in the house (toys, leash, etc.).

❑ Clean up after pets (in the yard).

❑ Clean off pets (when they come into the house).

❑ Clean pets' eating and drinking bowls regularly.

❑ Brush pets.

❑ Clean out litter box.

CLEANING DAY

❑ Deep clean eating area.

❑ Remove hair from furniture.

❑ Shake out pets' bedding.

DEEP CLEAN

❑ Bathe pets.

❑ Clean out doghouse.

❑ Wash pets' bedding.

Outside the Home
Cleaning Schedule Checklist

EVERYDAY CLEAN

❑ Pick up garbage.

❑ Put away sports and other equipment.

❑ Put garbage and recycling bins away.

❑ Put away garden tools.

CLEANING DAY

❑ Dust outside veranda.

❑ Sweep veranda and walkways.

❑ Wipe down garden furniture.

❑ Wash windows that need washing.

❑ Clean mailbox.

DEEP CLEAN

❑ Clean windows (check weather stripping and seals).

❑ Clean the exterior, including doors.

❑ Wash the veranda.

❑ Clean grills, patio furniture, and other seasonal equipment (summer and fall).

❑ Inspect and clean out garages, basements, lofts, and sheds.

Acknowledgments

This book was made possible through the dedication, experience, and knowledge of MOLLY MAID Franchise Owners and Home Service Professionals, who have been "sweeping up" since 1979. Thank you for your contribution.